INCOME TAXES 101

Money Saving Tax Tips Every Taxpayer Must Know

Stephanie Horne

Income Taxes 101: Money Saving Tax Tips Every Taxpayer Must Know

Copyright © 2018 by Stephanie Horne.

All Rights Reserved.

No part of this book may be reproduced in any form or by any electronic or mechanical means including information storage and retrieval systems without permission in writing from the author. The only exception is by a reviewer, who may quote short excerpts in a review.

The materials contained in this book are provided for general information purposes only and do not constitute legal or other professional advice on any subject matter. Stephanie Horne does not accept any responsibility for any loss which may arise from reliance on information contained in this book.

Visit my website at www.Bookkeeping-Basics.net

Printed in the United States of America
First Printing: Oct 2018
ISBN: 9781728675442

"You must pay taxes. But there's no law that says you gotta leave a tip."

—MORGAN STANLEY
ADVERTISEMENT

TABLE OF CONTENTS

ABOUT THE AUTHOR
INCOME TAX FILING

    Tax Facts
    Tax Forms
    Tax Deductions
    Tax Payments
    Tax Software
    Tax Professionals
    Tax Services
    Tax Resolution
    Tax Relief
    Tax Organizer
    Tax Worksheets

TAX FACTS AND TRIVIA

    Tax Trivia
    Tax Trivia Poll
    Tax Trivia Quiz
    Tax Trivia Quiz Answers
    Tax Accounting Test

INDIVIDUAL AND BUSINESS TAX FORMS

    Form 1040 For Individuals
    Schedule C For Small Business
    Schedule E for Rental Properties
    Schedule K1 1065 For Partnerships

INCOME TAX DEDUCTIONS

    Airline Personnel
    Business Professionals

- Day Care Providers
- Direct Sellers
- Educators
- Firefighters
- Hairstylist/Manicurists
- Law Enforcement Officers
- Long Haul Truckers
- Realtors
- Vehicle, Travel & Entertainment

ESTIMATED TAX PAYMENTS

- Corporations
- Individuals
- Payment Vouchers
- The No Refund Policy
- Adjusting Tax Payments

ACCOUNTING AND TAX SOFTWARE

- QuickBooks Premier
- QuickBooks Pro
- QuickBooks Online
- QuickBooks Point of Sale
- QuickBooks Accounting Software
- Online Income Taxes
- TurboTax Premier
- Turbotax Home and business
- H&R Block Deluxe
- H&R Block Business

INCOME TAX PROFESSIONALS

- Warning
- Tax Calculator
- Tax Reporting
- Hiring

TAX SERVICES

- Military Services
- Combat Pay
- Tax Prep Summary

INCOME TAX RESOLUTION

    Tax Solutions
    Income Tax Forms
    Income Tax Consultation

TAX RELIEF

    Military Tax Relief
    Disaster Assistance and Emergency Relief
    Innocent Spouse Relief

TAX ORGANIZER

    General Tax Organizer
    Pro-Forma Tax Organizer

EXCEL TAX WORKSHEETS

    Balance Sheet
    Small Profit and Loss
    Large Profit and Loss

ADDITIONAL RESOURCES
NOTES

ABOUT THE AUTHOR

Stephanie Horne, EA was born and raised in Northern California. She started her own at home bookkeeping and income tax preparation business in 2001 when she had her first child, a money saving website in 2018, and became an Enrolled Agent in 2014.

Her passion is in sharing her wealth of experience and knowledge with others to help ease their own journey both personally and financially by teaching them new financial and personal self-improvement skills

Her own individual journey has led to compiling this book that reveals many simple tax help techniques that anyone can apply immediately for a powerful, financial and business success transformation.

INCOME TAX FILING

Money Saving Liability Tips

*There's just one thing I can't
figure out. My income tax!*
—Nat King Cole

ARE YOU FEARFUL ABOUT MAKING costly mistakes on your income tax filing and missing out on personal and business deductions? Now you will no longer need to feel worried about expensive errors when it is time to file your income tax return. This book will give you advice on all the relevant tax information and deductions.

You will learn about what to look for when hiring tax preparation services versus doing your own income tax return, find out about interesting tax history & trivia, and get information about what is found on a tax organizer that will help you put together your annual tax information.

You will also learn about tax deductions and gain access to tax deduction lists for multiple different professions in addition to finding out about estimated tax payments, tax software, and income tax resolution options that are available should you ever run into an issue.

Information on how to handle tax liability payments along with reviews about accounting & tax software for doing your own income tax preparation can be found here as well.

TAX FACTS

Read about the history of taxes and interact with fun tax trivia, quizzes and tests about all things income tax related.

Do you think you are great at trivia? Prove it by taking the tax trivia dare right here, right now.

You are invited to take the challenge to find out how high you can score with a set of multiple-choice income tax questions that will also give you little known pieces of interesting knowledge.

TAX FORMS

IRS tax forms will provide you with explanations and examples of several of the main income and expense reporting documents.

We will take a look at Schedule C for small businesses, Schedule E for rental real estate properties, K-1 for estates, corporations and partnerships, along with form 1040 for individuals.

By walking through each of the line items and providing details regarding what should be included on each line, you will gain a greater understanding of what to do on your income tax filing

TAX DEDUCTIONS

Trying to determine your income tax deductions at tax time can leave you full of questions about what kinds of expenses are deductible.

While doing bookkeeping, and using income tax software, it is a really good idea to already know what these deductions are *before* tax time so that your chart of accounts can be set-up accordingly.

TAX PAYMENTS

Should you adjust your estimated tax payment if business is suddenly more or less than usual? Any kind of economic slowdown will affect businesses in all industries, from service to retail, causing many companies to re-evaluate their financial and tax situation.

If business is slower than normal, you may want to consider adjusting your quarterly estimated tax payment vouchers.

TAX SOFTWARE

You can organize your personal and business finances quickly and easily with QuickBooks tax software. In addition, you can get quick access to everyday tasks like invoicing, bill tracking, check-writing and payroll.

You can also track sales and expenses, share your data with Microsoft Excel and your accountant, as well as save time completing routine tasks and paperwork enabling you to spend more time on your business.

TAX PROFESSIONALS

A recent IRS report has highlighted the need for honest tax professionals, because many tax "experts" are leaving their clients at risk of serious penalties.

Is your current tax professional putting you at risk? Like most Americans, you probably want to receive a larger refund from the IRS. And you should be aware of every tax deduction that you can legally take advantage of.

However, some people either unknowingly or intentionally try to take advantage of income tax deductions that they shouldn't be receiving, which get them into major trouble with the IRS.

TAX SERVICES

May is National Military Appreciation Month, and the Internal Revenue Service wants members of the military and their families to know about the many tax benefits available to them.

Each year, the IRS publishes Publication 3, Armed Forces Tax Guide, a free booklet packed with valuable information and tips designed to help service members and their families take advantage of all tax benefits allowed by law.

TAX RESOLUTION

Get income tax resolution help with clearing up your disputes, penalties, interest and back taxes owed here.

It can be very scary and stressful when you are experiencing income tax liability issues and don't know where to go or what to do to help resolve the problem.

We are here to help you through the process of clearing everything up in the quickest, easiest, most cost efficient and stress free manner possible.

TAX RELIEF

Did you know tax relief is available to help lower your tax liabilities? Find out how to obtain tax help through Military Relief, Innocent Spouse Relief, Disaster and Emergency Assistant Relief.

After Congress successfully got through a one-year patch and reached the serious consideration stage, the now annual tax extenders packages are poised waiting for the right moment to jump onto the legislative bandwagon.

TAX ORGANIZER

A tax organizer can help by facilitating the process of pulling together your tax information. This basic organizer is designed for new tax or bookkeeping clients and allows you to enter your information right on the screen.

You can then print the completed organizer and fax, mail or hand-deliver it to the office. Current clients should contact the office to request a pro-forma organizer that includes prior year information and carryover data.

TAX WORKSHEETS

There are convenient excel bookkeeping templates that are great for when you don't want to spend a lot of money on accounting software when first getting started.

Rather than having to purchase bookkeeping software, you can start now with your existing excel software by using these free and inexpensive excel bookkeeping worksheets for sole proprietor or rental real estate transactions.

TAX FACTS AND TRIVIA

Fun Trivia, Quizzes & Tests

There is nothing new in the world except the history you do not know.
—Harry S Truman

READ AND INTERACT WITH THESE fun tax trivia bookkeeping basics income tax facts, quizzes and tests about all things income tax history related. Do you think you are great at trivia? Prove it by taking the tax trivia dare right here right now.

You are invited to take the challenge to find out how high you can score with a set of multiple choice income tax questions that will give you little known pieces of interesting knowledge while you are at it.

You can go ahead and dive right in to one of the trivia dare quizzes and tests, or you can read up on some interesting income tax facts here to freshen up before you begin.

TAX TRIVIA

Did you know...

1) An extremely important artifact, the Rosetta Stone, was the main key to the ultimate deciphering of ancient Egyptian hieroglyphics... and the writing found in it is mostly about taxes.

2) The Roman emperor taxed urine in the 1st century. It was used to launder garments as well as collected for the ammonia.

3) The country of Romania was trying to get itself out of a major recession in 2011, so they decided to add a new profession to the country's labor code which would make it subject to taxation. The new profession added was Witchcraft.

4) This is a story about the stripper who ended up in tax court after attempting to deduct her

boob job as a medical deduction. Her name was Cynthia Hess (otherwise known as Chesty Love).

The IRS originally disallowed the deduction because cosmetic surgery that isn't being done to correct a disfigurement or for some other life-saving purpose is not deductible.

However, the higher court ended up allowing the expense instead as a legitimate ordinary and necessary business expense.

5) There are many European nations that have a tax on cow flatulence. It's really important to them because methane gas is one of the main greenhouse gases that can cause climate change. For real... cow flatulence!

6. The Russian Emperor Peter the Great taxed beards because he wanted men to be clean shaven.

7. There have at times been over 7 million words in the tax law and regulations. This amount totally outnumbers The Bible, Declaration of Independence and the Gettysburg Address all combined together.

TAX TRIVIA POLL

This is a quick yes, no or maybe so tax trivia question and answer poll asking all kinds of interesting questions to do with your personal integrity.

Be totally honest and see how you match up in relation to your peers when you take the test online at bookkeeping-basics.net/tax-trivia.html.

Tax Trivia Poll

Have You Ever Exaggerated On Your Tax Return?

Have You Ever Fibbed About Your Income?

Have You Ever Fibbed About Your Mileage?

Have You Ever Deducted A Personal Meal As A Business Meal And Entertainment Expense?

Have You Ever Fibbed About Education Expenses?

Have You Ever Fibbed About Charitable Expenses?

Have You Ever Intentionally Left Info Off A Return?

Have You Ever Spitefully Taken An Ex Spouse's Child Deduction From Them Without Asking?

Have You Ever Filed A Tax Return Over A Year Late?

Have You Ever Lied About Being Head Of Household?

TAX TRIVIA QUIZ

This first Trivia Quiz is a simple 5 question multiple choice series of questions that will rate you on a scale of 1 through 3 based on the answers you provide when you take it online at bookkeeping-basics.net/tax-trivia.html. The scale will also provide detailed descriptions for what your rating means in relation to how well you know your income tax facts.

Tax Trivia Quiz

5 Quick Multiple Choice Questions With Answers

1. Why Did Tax Day Become April 15th?

☐ To Help Accountants

☐ To Help Tax Payers

☐ To Help The IRS

☐ All Of The Above

2. A Tax Preparer Was Considered The Most Noble Person In Which Ancient Civilization?

☐ Carthage

☐ Egypt

☐ Greece

☐ Mesopotamia

3. During World War I What Was The Top Income Tax Rate?

☐ 77%

☐ 55%

☐ 33%

☐ 22%

4. What Is The Largest Expense At A State Level?

☐ Education System

☐ Healthcare

☐ Public Help

☐ Transportation

5. How Much Do Taxpayers Tend To Pay Per Every $100 Taken By The Federal Government?

☐ $0.41

☐ $0.99

☐ $1.49

☐ $2.25

TAX TRIVIA QUIZ ANSWERS

1. All of the above

2. Greece

3. 77%

4. Healthcare

5. $0.41

How well did you do on the quiz?

5 correct: Outstanding job! You have obviously been doing your homework. You seem to have a good handle on your tax trivia and are a pro when it comes to your income tax history knowledge!

3-4 correct: Good work. You definitely have a good start on knowing your income tax trivia. If you continue your tax history education, you may be able to score a 100% next time.

However, you will still want to make sure that

you have a good income tax mentor to help answer any questions you may have as new things come up.

0-2 correct: Need help. You should seriously consider hiring a professional income tax preparer to help with your income tax needs. You probably have other priorities than to do your own income taxes.

If you enjoyed this free tax trivia quiz or would like something a bit more substantial, check out the more comprehensive 20 question interactive bookkeeping tax test next at bookkeeping-basics.net/bookkeeping-test.html. It is in video format so there is no need to write anything down.

TAX ACCOUNTING TEST

Your financials are a very important aspect of your business. Whether you are a business owner or bookkeeper, it is a good idea to evaluate your candidates or yourself with a tax accounting and bookkeeping exam such as this one in order to ensure you are getting or providing qualified, accurate bookkeeping expertise.

Missing skills can lead to costly mistakes, and there is no need to take chances. Recording the daily financial transactions of a business requires more than just knowledge of bookkeeping software such as QuickBooks.

This tax accounting exam can help to assess a candidates' knowledge of accounting fundamentals, from general ledger, inventory, payroll, accounts payable & accounts receivable, to invoices and financial reports.

The tax accounting test will make sure that you will no longer need to rely only on the interview to detect exaggerations in skills and knowledge that are sometimes found in resumes.

Pre-employment accounting tests from bookkeeping-basics.net are a smart choice for assessing a candidates true level of skills working with accounts payable & receivables, debits and credits, payroll, and financial statements such as the balance sheet and profit and loss statement.

1. Determine the bookkeeping skill levels of your candidates or yourself before the interview.
2. Improve your efficiency in recruiting qualified bookkeepers with accounting and bookkeeping exams designed by experts in the field.
3. Use one practical and concise test to evaluate many different bookkeeping skill categories

The interactive tax accounting test is presented as a video with both multiple choice and true and false type questions.

Simply read the question and click on the choice that you think is correct then click next until you reach the last question. You can go back and review questions before submitting.

Once submitted you will receive immediate access to the total score or number of questions that were answered correctly out of 20.

You will also have the ability to scroll through each of the questions to see exactly which questions were missed and what the correct answer should have been.

INDIVIDUAL AND BUSINESS TAX FORMS

Form 1040, Sch C, Sch E, & K1

The last time the government tried to make taxes easier, it created a 1040 EZ form with a 52 page help booklet.
—Brad D Smith

INCOME TAX PREPARATION FORM 1040 is the primary personal income tax report that is used for declaring the summary total of all personal and business income and deductible expenses for each year.

FORM 1040 FOR INDIVIDUALS

Starting in 2018 there have been many changes made to the format of form 1040. The early release draft shows that it will now be made up of the following primary features:

- Name, Address, Tax Identification Number, Dependents
- Wages, Salaries, Tips, Etc. (W-2 Employee Earnings)
- Interest Income (1099-INT)
- Dividend Income (1099-DIV)
- IRA, Pensions, and Annuities (1099-R)
- Social Security Benefits (SSA)
- Standard or Itemized Deductions
- Qualified Business Income Deductions

- Child Tax Credits
- Other Taxes
- Federal Income Tax Withheld From Forms W-2 and 1099
- Refundable Credits (EIC, Sch 8812, Form 8863)
- Amount To Be Refunded or Amount Owed
- Routing and Account Number
- Estimated Penalty
- Signature

Following is a draft 2018 form 1040:

Caution: *DRAFT—NOT FOR FILING*

This is an early release draft of the 2018 IRS Form 1040, U.S. Individual Income Tax Return, which the IRS is providing for your information, review, and comment. **Do not file draft forms.** Also, do not rely on draft forms, instructions, and publications for filing. We generally do not release drafts of forms until we believe we have incorporated all changes, and we do not expect this draft to change significantly before being published as final. Forms generally are subject to OMB approval before they can be officially released. Early release drafts are at IRS.gov/DraftForms, and may remain there even after the final release is posted at IRS.gov/LatestForms. All information about forms, instructions, and publications is at IRS.gov/Forms.

Also, note that almost every form and publication also has its own page on IRS.gov. For example, the Form 1040 page is at IRS.gov/Form1040; a Form W-8BEN-E page is at IRS.gov/W8BENE; the Publication 17 page is at IRS.gov/Pub17; the Form W-4 page is at IRS.gov/W4; and the Schedule A (Form 1040) page is at IRS.gov/ScheduleA. If typing in a link instead of clicking on it, be sure to type the link into the address bar of your browser, not in a Search box. Note that these are friendly shortcut links that will automatically redirect to the actual link for the page.

If you wish, you can submit comments about this draft Form 1040 and/or its 6 new numbered schedules to WI.1040.Comments@IRS.gov. We cannot respond to all comments due to the high volume we receive. Please note that we may not be able to consider some suggestions until the 2019 revisions.

Form 1040 Department of the Treasury—Internal Revenue Service (99)
U.S. Individual Income Tax Return 2018   OMB No. 1545-0074   IRS Use Only—Do not write or staple in this space.

Filing status: ☐ Single ☐ Married filing jointly ☐ Married filing separately ☐ Head of household ☐ Qualifying widow(er)

Your first name and initial | Last name | Your social security number

Your standard deduction: ☐ Someone can claim you as a dependent ☐ You were born before January 2, 1954 ☐ You are blind

If joint return, spouse's first name and initial | Last name | Spouse's social security number

Spouse standard deduction: ☐ Someone can claim your spouse as a dependent ☐ Spouse was born before January 2, 1954 ☐ Full-year health care coverage or exempt (see inst.)
☐ Spouse is blind ☐ Spouse itemizes on a separate return or you were dual-status alien

Home address (number and street). If you have a P.O. box, see instructions. | Apt. no. | Presidential Election Campaign (see inst.) ☐ You ☐ Spouse

City, town or post office, state, and ZIP code. If you have a foreign address, attach Schedule 6. | If more than four dependents, see inst. and ✓ here ▶ ☐

Dependents (see instructions):
(1) First name Last name	(2) Social security number	(3) Relationship to you	(4) ✓ If qualifies for (see inst.):
			Child tax credit / Credit for other dependents
			☐ ☐
			☐ ☐
			☐ ☐
			☐ ☐

Sign Here
Joint return? See instructions. Keep a copy for your records.

Under penalties of perjury, I declare that I have examined this return and accompanying schedules and statements, and to the best of my knowledge and belief, they are true, correct, and complete. Declaration of preparer (other than taxpayer) is based on all information of which preparer has any knowledge.

Your signature | Date | Your occupation | If the IRS sent you an Identity Protection PIN, enter it here (see inst.)

Spouse's signature. If a joint return, **both** must sign. | Date | Spouse's occupation | If the IRS sent you an Identity Protection PIN, enter it here (see inst.)

Paid Preparer Use Only
Preparer's name | Preparer's signature | PTIN | Firm's EIN | Check if: ☐ 3rd Party Designee
Firm's name ▶ | | Phone no. | | ☐ Self-employed
Firm's address ▶

For Disclosure, Privacy Act, and Paperwork Reduction Act Notice, see separate instructions.   Cat. No. 11320B   Form **1040** (2018)

Form 1040 (2018) Page **2**

Attach Form(s) W-2. Also attach Form(s) W-2G and 1099-R if tax was withheld.	1	Wages, salaries, tips, etc. Attach Form(s) W-2			1	
	2a	Tax-exempt interest	2a	b Taxable interest	2b	
	3a	Qualified dividends	3a	b Ordinary dividends	3b	
	4a	IRAs, pensions, and annuities	4a	b Taxable amount	4b	
	5a	Social security benefits	5a	b Taxable amount	5b	
	6	Total income. Add lines 1 through 5. Add any amount from Schedule 1, line 22			6	
	7	Adjusted gross income. If you have no adjustments to income, enter the amount from line 6; otherwise, subtract Schedule 1, line 36, from line 6			7	
Standard Deduction for— • Single or married filing separately, $12,000 • Married filing jointly or Qualifying widow(er), $24,000 • Head of household, $18,000 • If you checked any box under Standard deduction, see instructions.	8	Standard deduction or itemized deductions (from Schedule A)			8	
	9	Qualified business income deduction (see instructions)			9	
	10	Taxable income. Subtract lines 8 and 9 from line 7. If zero or less, enter -0-			10	
	11	a Tax (see inst) _____ (check if any from: 1 ☐ Form(s) 8814 2 ☐ Form 4972 3 ☐ _____) b Add any amount from Schedule 2 and check here ▶ ☐			11	
	12	a Child tax credit/credit for other dependents _____ b Add any amount from Schedule 3 and check here ▶ ☐			12	
	13	Subtract line 12 from line 11. If zero or less, enter -0-			13	
	14	Other taxes. Attach Schedule 4			14	
	15	Total tax. Add lines 13 and 14			15	
	16	Federal income tax withheld from Forms W-2 and 1099			16	
	17	Refundable credits: a EIC (see inst.) _____ b Sch 8812 _____ c Form 8863 _____ Add any amount from Schedule 5 _____			17	
	18	Add lines 16 and 17. These are your total payments			18	
Refund Direct deposit? See instructions.	19	If line 18 is more than line 15, subtract line 15 from line 18. This is the amount you **overpaid**			19	
	20a	Amount of line 19 you want **refunded to you.** If Form 8888 is attached, check here ▶ ☐			20a	
	▶ b	Routing number _____ ▶ c Type: ☐ Checking ☐ Savings				
	▶ d	Account number _____				
	21	Amount of line 19 you want applied to your 2019 estimated tax ▶	21			
Amount You Owe	22	**Amount you owe.** Subtract line 18 from line 15. For details on how to pay, see instructions ▶			22	
	23	Estimated tax penalty (see instructions) ▶	23			

Go to *www.irs.gov/Form1040* for instructions and the latest information.

Form **1040** (2018)

SCHEDULE C FOR SMALL BUSINESS

You should use Schedule C for small business when reporting income or loss from a business that you operated or a service you provided as a sole proprietor.

Activities that qualify as a business are those you are engaged in for income or profit on a regular and continual basis. The form is made up of the following items:

- Name, Tax ID, Business Code, Business Name, Address
- Accounting Method (Cash, Accrual)
- Gross Sales and Receipts (all income from business activities)
- Cost of Goods Sold (Materials, Labor)
- Expenses (Advertising, Car, Computer, Office Furniture, Depreciation, Shredder Equipment, Insurance, Interest, Lighting, Legal & Professional, Office Supplies, Rent or Lease, Repairs & Maintenance, Taxes & Licenses, Travel, Meals & Entertainment, Utilities, Wages)
- Business Use of Home
- Net Profit or Loss

Following is a sample 2017 Schedule C:

SCHEDULE C (Form 1040)
Department of the Treasury
Internal Revenue Service (99)

Profit or Loss From Business
(Sole Proprietorship)
▶ Go to *www.irs.gov/ScheduleC* for instructions and the latest information.
▶ Attach to Form 1040, 1040NR, or 1041; partnerships generally must file Form 1065.

OMB No. 1545-0074
2017
Attachment Sequence No. 09

Name of proprietor | Social security number (SSN)

A Principal business or profession, including product or service (see instructions)
B Enter code from instructions ▶

C Business name. If no separate business name, leave blank.
D Employer ID number (EIN) (see instr.)

E Business address (including suite or room no.) ▶
City, town or post office, state, and ZIP code

F Accounting method: (1) ☐ Cash (2) ☐ Accrual (3) ☐ Other (specify) ▶
G Did you "materially participate" in the operation of this business during 2017? If "No," see instructions for limit on losses . ☐ Yes ☐ No
H If you started or acquired this business during 2017, check here ▶ ☐
I Did you make any payments in 2017 that would require you to file Form(s) 1099? (see instructions) . . . . ☐ Yes ☐ No
J If "Yes," did you or will you file required Forms 1099? . . . . ☐ Yes ☐ No

Part I Income

1	Gross receipts or sales. See instructions for line 1 and check the box if this income was reported to you on Form W-2 and the "Statutory employee" box on that form was checked . . . . ▶ ☐	1
2	Returns and allowances	2
3	Subtract line 2 from line 1	3
4	Cost of goods sold (from line 42)	4
5	**Gross profit.** Subtract line 4 from line 3	5
6	Other income, including federal and state gasoline or fuel tax credit or refund (see instructions)	6
7	**Gross income.** Add lines 5 and 6 . . . . ▶	7

Part II Expenses. Enter expenses for business use of your home *only* on line 30.

8	Advertising	8		18	Office expense (see instructions)	18
9	Car and truck expenses (see instructions)	9		19	Pension and profit-sharing plans	19
10	Commissions and fees .	10		20	Rent or lease (see instructions):	
11	Contract labor (see instructions)	11		a	Vehicles, machinery, and equipment	20a
12	Depletion	12		b	Other business property . . .	20b
13	Depreciation and section 179 expense deduction (not included in Part III) (see instructions)	13		21	Repairs and maintenance . . .	21
				22	Supplies (not included in Part III) .	22
				23	Taxes and licenses	23
				24	Travel, meals, and entertainment:	
14	Employee benefit programs (other than on line 19) . .	14		a	Travel	24a
15	Insurance (other than health)	15		b	Deductible meals and entertainment (see instructions)	24b
16	Interest:			25	Utilities	25
a	Mortgage (paid to banks, etc.)	16a		26	Wages (less employment credits) .	26
b	Other	16b		27a	Other expenses (from line 48) . .	27a
17	Legal and professional services	17		b	**Reserved for future use** . . .	27b
28	**Total expenses** before expenses for business use of home. Add lines 8 through 27a . . . . . . ▶					28
29	Tentative profit or (loss). Subtract line 28 from line 7					29
30	Expenses for business use of your home. Do not report these expenses elsewhere. Attach Form 8829 unless using the simplified method (see instructions).					
	Simplified method filers only: enter the total square footage of: (a) your home: _____ and (b) the part of your home used for business: _____. Use the Simplified Method Worksheet in the instructions to figure the amount to enter on line 30					30
31	**Net profit or (loss).** Subtract line 30 from line 29.					
	• If a profit, enter on **both** **Form 1040, line 12** (or **Form 1040NR, line 13**) and on **Schedule SE, line 2.** (If you checked the box on line 1, see instructions). Estates and trusts, enter on **Form 1041, line 3.**					31
	• If a loss, you **must** go to line 32.					
32	If you have a loss, check the box that describes your investment in this activity (see instructions).					
	• If you checked 32a, enter the loss on **both Form 1040, line 12,** (or **Form 1040NR, line 13**) and on **Schedule SE, line 2.** (If you checked the box on line 1, see the line 31 instructions). Estates and trusts, enter on **Form 1041, line 3.**				32a ☐	All investment is at risk.
	• If you checked 32b, you **must** attach **Form 6198.** Your loss may be limited.				32b ☐	Some investment is not at risk.

For Paperwork Reduction Act Notice, see the separate instructions.   Cat. No. 11334P   Schedule C (Form 1040) 2017

Schedule C (Form 1040) 2017   Page **2**

Part III Cost of Goods Sold (see instructions)

33 Method(s) used to value closing inventory: **a** ☐ Cost   **b** ☐ Lower of cost or market   **c** ☐ Other (attach explanation)

34 Was there any change in determining quantities, costs, or valuations between opening and closing inventory? If "Yes," attach explanation . . . . ☐ Yes ☐ No

35 Inventory at beginning of year. If different from last year's closing inventory, attach explanation **35**

36 Purchases less cost of items withdrawn for personal use **36**

37 Cost of labor. Do not include any amounts paid to yourself **37**

38 Materials and supplies **38**

39 Other costs **39**

40 Add lines 35 through 39 . . . . **40**

41 Inventory at end of year **41**

42 **Cost of goods sold.** Subtract line 41 from line 40. Enter the result here and on line 4 . . . . . . **42**

Part IV Information on Your Vehicle. Complete this part **only** if you are claiming car or truck expenses on line 9 and are not required to file Form 4562 for this business. See the instructions for line 13 to find out if you must file Form 4562.

43 When did you place your vehicle in service for business purposes? (month, day, year) ▶ ___/___/___

44 Of the total number of miles you drove your vehicle during 2017, enter the number of miles you used your vehicle for:

a Business _____   **b** Commuting (see instructions) _____   **c** Other _____

45 Was your vehicle available for personal use during off-duty hours? . . . . ☐ Yes ☐ No

46 Do you (or your spouse) have another vehicle available for personal use? . . . . ☐ Yes ☐ No

47a Do you have evidence to support your deduction? . . . . ☐ Yes ☐ No

  b If "Yes," is the evidence written? . . . . ☐ Yes ☐ No

Part V Other Expenses. List below business expenses not included on lines 8–26 or line 30.

_____   _____

_____   _____

_____   _____

_____   _____

_____   _____

_____   _____

_____   _____

_____   _____

_____   _____

48 Total other expenses. Enter here and on line 27a **48**

SCHEDULE E FOR RENTAL PROPERTIES

Schedule E is the tax form that is used for rental real estate properties to report income and loss from rentals, royalties, partnerships, S-corporations, estates and trusts.

The 2018 draft copy of the Schedule E shows the following attributes:

- Name, Tax ID, Property Address, Type of Property
- Days Rented, Personal Days
- Rents/Royalties Received
- Expenses (Advertising, Auto & Travel, Cleaning and Maintenance, Commissions, Insurance, Legal and Professional Fees, Management Fees, Interest, Repairs, Supplies, Taxes, Utilities, Depreciation, Other)
- Summary Of All Properties
- Income or Loss From Partnerships and S Corporations
- Income or Loss From Estates and Trusts
- Income or Loss From REMICs

Following is a draft of the 2018 Schedule E:

Caution: *DRAFT—NOT FOR FILING*

This is an early release draft of an IRS tax form, instructions, or publication, which the IRS is providing for your information as a courtesy. **Do not file draft forms.** Also, do not rely on draft forms, instructions, and publications for filing. We generally do not release drafts of forms until we believe we have incorporated all changes. However, unexpected issues sometimes arise, or legislation is passed, necessitating a change to a draft form. In addition, forms generally are subject to OMB approval before they can be officially released. Drafts of instructions and publications usually have at least some changes before being officially released.

Early release drafts are at IRS.gov/DraftForms, and may remain there even after the final release is posted at IRS.gov/DownloadForms. All information about all forms, instructions, and pubs is at IRS.gov/Forms.

Almost every form and publication also has its own page on IRS.gov. For example, the Form 1040 page is at IRS.gov/Form1040; the Publication 17 page is at IRS.gov/Pub17; the Form W-4 page is at IRS.gov/W4; and the Schedule A (Form 1040) page is at IRS.gov/ScheduleA. If typing in a link above instead of clicking on it, be sure to type the link into the address bar of your browser, not in a Search box. Note that these are friendly shortcut links that will automatically go to the actual link for the page.

If you wish, you can submit comments about draft or final forms, instructions, or publications at IRS.gov/FormsComments. We cannot respond to all comments due to the high volume we receive. Please note that we may not be able to consider many suggestions until the subsequent revision of the product.

SCHEDULE E
(Form 1040)

Department of the Treasury
Internal Revenue Service (99)

Supplemental Income and Loss
(From rental real estate, royalties, partnerships, S corporations, estates, trusts, REMICs, etc.)

▶ Attach to Form 1040, 1040NR, or Form 1041.
▶ Go to *www.irs.gov/ScheduleE* for instructions and the latest information.

OMB No. 1545-0074

2018

Attachment Sequence No. **13**

Name(s) shown on return

Your social security number

DRAFT AS OF July 16, 2018 DO NOT FILE

Part I — Income or Loss From Rental Real Estate and Royalties
Note: If you are in the business of renting personal property, use **Schedule C or C-EZ** (see instructions). If you are an individual, report farm rental income or loss from **Form 4835** on page 2, line 40.

A	Did you make any payments in 2018 that would require you to file Form(s) 1099? (see instructions)	☐ Yes ☐ No
B	If "Yes," did you or will you file required Forms 1099?	☐ Yes ☐ No

1a Physical address of each property (street, city, state, ZIP code)

A _____
B _____
C _____

1b	Type of Property (from list below)	2 For each rental real estate property listed above, report the number of fair rental and personal use days. Check the QJV box only if you meet the requirements to file as a qualified joint venture. See instructions.		Fair Rental Days	Personal Use Days	QJV
A			A			☐
B			B			☐
C			C			☐

Type of Property:
1 Single Family Residence   3 Vacation/Short-Term Rental   5 Land   7 Self-Rental
2 Multi-Family Residence   4 Commercial   6 Royalties   8 Other (describe)

Income:	Properties:		A	B	C
3	Rents received	3			
4	Royalties received	4			
Expenses:					
5	Advertising	5			
6	Auto and travel (see instructions)	6			
7	Cleaning and maintenance	7			
8	Commissions	8			
9	Insurance	9			
10	Legal and other professional fees	10			
11	Management fees	11			
12	Mortgage interest paid to banks, etc. (see instructions)	12			
13	Other interest	13			
14	Repairs	14			
15	Supplies	15			
16	Taxes	16			
17	Utilities	17			
18	Depreciation expense or depletion	18			
19	Other (list) ▶ _____	19			
20	Total expenses. Add lines 5 through 19 . . .	20			
21	Subtract line 20 from line 3 (rents) and/or 4 (royalties). If result is a (loss), see instructions to find out if you must file **Form 6198**	21			
22	Deductible rental real estate loss after limitation, if any, on **Form 8582** (see instructions)	22	( )	( )	( )

23a	Total of all amounts reported on line 3 for all rental properties	23a	
b	Total of all amounts reported on line 4 for all royalty properties	23b	
c	Total of all amounts reported on line 12 for all properties	23c	
d	Total of all amounts reported on line 18 for all properties	23d	
e	Total of all amounts reported on line 20 for all properties	23e	
24	**Income.** Add positive amounts shown on line 21. **Do not** include any losses	24	
25	**Losses.** Add royalty losses from line 21 and rental real estate losses from line 22. Enter total losses here .	25	( )
26	**Total rental real estate and royalty income or (loss).** Combine lines 24 and 25. Enter the result here. If Parts II, III, IV, and line 40 on page 2 do not apply to you, also enter this amount on Schedule 1 (Form 1040), line 17, or Form 1040NR, line 18. Otherwise, include this amount in the total on line 41 on page 2	26	

For Paperwork Reduction Act Notice, see the separate instructions.   Cat. No. 11344L   Schedule E (Form 1040) 2018

Schedule E (Form 1040) 2018   Attachment Sequence No. **13**   Page **2**

Name(s) shown on return. Do not enter name and social security number if shown on other side.   Your social security number

Caution: The IRS compares amounts reported on your tax return with amounts shown on Schedule(s) K-1.

Part II Income or Loss From Partnerships and S Corporations — Note: If you report a loss, receive a distribution, dispose of stock, or receive a loan repayment from an S corporation, you **must** check the box in column **(e)** on line 28 and attach the required basis computation. If you report a loss from an at-risk activity for which **any** amount is **not** at risk, you **must** check the box in column **(f)** on line 28 and attach **Form 6198** (see instructions).

27 Are you reporting any loss not allowed in a prior year due to the at-risk, excess farm loss, or basis limitations, a prior year unallowed loss from a passive activity (if that loss was not reported on Form 8582), or unreimbursed partnership expenses? If you answered "Yes," see instructions before completing this section . . . . ☐ Yes ☐ No

28

	(a) Name	(b) Enter P for partnership; S for S corporation	(c) Check if foreign partnership	(d) Employer identification number	(e) Check if basis computation is required	(f) Check if any amount is not at risk
A			☐		☐	☐
B			☐		☐	☐
C			☐		☐	☐
D			☐		☐	☐

	Passive Income and Loss			Nonpassive Income and Loss		
	(g) Passive loss allowed (attach **Form 8582** if required)	(h) Passive income from **Schedule K-1**		(i) Nonpassive loss from **Schedule K-1**	(j) Section 179 expense deduction from **Form 4562**	(k) Nonpassive income from **Schedule K-1**
A						
B						
C						
D						

29a Totals

 b Totals

30 Add columns (h) and (k) of line 29a. **30**

31 Add columns (g), (i), and (j) of line 29b. . . . . **31** ( )

32 **Total partnership and S corporation income or (loss).** Combine lines 30 and 31 . . . . . **32**

Part III Income or Loss From Estates and Trusts

33

	(a) Name	(b) Employer identification number
A		
B		

	Passive Income and Loss		Nonpassive Income and Loss	
	(c) Passive deduction or loss allowed (attach **Form 8582** if required)	(d) Passive income from **Schedule K-1**	(e) Deduction or loss from **Schedule K-1**	(f) Other income from **Schedule K-1**
A				
B				

34a Totals

 b Totals

35 Add columns (d) and (f) of line 34a **35**

36 Add columns (c) and (e) of line 34b . . . . **36** ( )

37 **Total estate and trust income or (loss).** Combine lines 35 and 36 . . . . **37**

Part IV Income or Loss From Real Estate Mortgage Investment Conduits (REMICs) — Residual Holder

38

	(a) Name	(b) Employer identification number	(c) Excess inclusion from **Schedules Q,** line 2c (see instructions)	(d) Taxable income (net loss) from **Schedules Q,** line 1b	(e) Income from **Schedules Q,** line 3b

39 Combine columns (d) and (e) only. Enter the result here and include in the total on line 41 below . **39**

Part V Summary

40 Net farm rental income or (loss) from **Form 4835.** Also, complete line 42 below **40**

41 Total income or (loss). Combine lines 26, 32, 37, 39, and 40. Enter the result here and on Schedule 1 (Form 1040), line 17, or Form 1040NR, line 18 ▶ **41**

42 **Reconciliation of farming and fishing income.** Enter your gross farming and fishing income reported on Form 4835, line 7; Schedule K-1 (Form 1065), box 14, code B; Schedule K-1 (Form 1120S), box 17, code AC; and Schedule K-1 (Form 1041), box 14, code F (see instructions) . **42**

43 **Reconciliation for real estate professionals.** If you were a real estate professional (see instructions), enter the net income or (loss) you reported anywhere on Form 1040 or Form 1040NR from all rental real estate activities in which you materially participated under the passive activity loss rules . **43**

Schedule E (Form 1040) 2018

SCHEDULE K1 1065 FOR PARTNERSHIPS

Schedule K-1, Form 1065 is a tax document that is issued for an investment in partnership interests. The purpose is to report your share of the partnership's income, deductions and credits.

It is issued around the same time as Form 1099 and serves a similar tax reporting purpose. The main items you will find on the Schedule K-1 are:

- Partnership Tax ID, Name, Address, PTP
- General, Limited, Domestic or Foreign Status
- Beginning and Ending Profit, Loss & Capital %
- Partner's Share of Income, Deductions & Credits
- Ordinary Income, Rental Real Estate, Guaranteed Payments, Interest Income, Dividends, Royalties, Capital Gains & Losses, Collectibles, Section 179 Deduction, Self-Employment Earnings, Credits, Distributions

Following is sample 2017 Schedule K-1:

651117

| ☐ Final K-1 | ☐ Amended K-1 | OMB No. 1545-0123 |

Schedule K-1 (Form 1065) 2017
Department of the Treasury
Internal Revenue Service
For calendar year 2017, or tax year
beginning ___ / ___ / 2017 ending ___ / ___ / ___

Partner's Share of Income, Deductions, Credits, etc. ▶ See back of form and separate instructions.

Part I Information About the Partnership

A Partnership's employer identification number

B Partnership's name, address, city, state, and ZIP code

C IRS Center where partnership filed return

D ☐ Check if this is a publicly traded partnership (PTP)

Part II Information About the Partner

E Partner's identifying number

F Partner's name, address, city, state, and ZIP code

G ☐ General partner or LLC member-manager   ☐ Limited partner or other LLC member

H ☐ Domestic partner   ☐ Foreign partner

I1 What type of entity is this partner? _____

I2 If this partner is a retirement plan (IRA/SEP/Keogh/etc.), check here ☐

J Partner's share of profit, loss, and capital (see instructions):
	Beginning	Ending
Profit	%	%
Loss	%	%
Capital	%	%

K Partner's share of liabilities at year end:
Nonrecourse . . . . . . $ _____
Qualified nonrecourse financing . $ _____
Recourse . . . . $ _____

L Partner's capital account analysis:
Beginning capital account . . . $ _____
Capital contributed during the year $ _____
Current year increase (decrease) . $ _____
Withdrawals & distributions . . . $ (_____)
Ending capital account . . . . $ _____

☐ Tax basis   ☐ GAAP   ☐ Section 704(b) book
☐ Other (explain)

M Did the partner contribute property with a built-in gain or loss?
☐ Yes   ☐ No
If "Yes," attach statement (see instructions)

Part III Partner's Share of Current Year Income, Deductions, Credits, and Other Items

1	Ordinary business income (loss)	15	Credits
2	Net rental real estate income (loss)		
3	Other net rental income (loss)	16	Foreign transactions
4	Guaranteed payments		
5	Interest income		
6a	Ordinary dividends		
6b	Qualified dividends		
7	Royalties		
8	Net short-term capital gain (loss)		
9a	Net long-term capital gain (loss)	17	Alternative minimum tax (AMT) items
9b	Collectibles (28%) gain (loss)		
9c	Unrecaptured section 1250 gain		
10	Net section 1231 gain (loss)	18	Tax-exempt income and nondeductible expenses
11	Other income (loss)		
		19	Distributions
12	Section 179 deduction		
13	Other deductions	20	Other information
14	Self-employment earnings (loss)		

*See attached statement for additional information.

For Paperwork Reduction Act Notice, see Instructions for Form 1065.   www.irs.gov/Form1065   Cat. No. 11394R   Schedule K-1 (Form 1065) 2017

Schedule K-1 (Form 1065) 2017 — Page 2

This list identifies the codes used on Schedule K-1 for all partners and provides summarized reporting information for partners who file Form 1040. For detailed reporting and filing information, see the separate Partner's Instructions for Schedule K-1 and the instructions for your income tax return.

1. **Ordinary business income (loss).** Determine whether the income (loss) is passive or nonpassive and enter on your return as follows.

	Report on
Passive loss	See the Partner's Instructions
Passive income	Schedule E, line 28, column (g)
Nonpassive loss	See the Partner's Instructions
Nonpassive income	Schedule E, line 28, column (j)

2. **Net rental real estate income (loss)** — See the Partner's Instructions
3. **Other net rental income (loss)**
   - Net income — Schedule E, line 28, column (g)
   - Net loss — See the Partner's Instructions
4. **Guaranteed payments** — Schedule E, line 28, column (j)
5. **Interest income** — Form 1040, line 8a
6a. **Ordinary dividends** — Form 1040, line 9a
6b. **Qualified dividends** — Form 1040, line 9b
7. **Royalties** — Schedule E, line 4
8. **Net short-term capital gain (loss)** — Schedule D, line 5
9a. **Net long-term capital gain (loss)** — Schedule D, line 12
9b. **Collectibles (28%) gain (loss)** — 28% Rate Gain Worksheet, line 4 (Schedule D instructions)
9c. **Unrecaptured section 1250 gain** — See the Partner's Instructions
10. **Net section 1231 gain (loss)** — See the Partner's Instructions
11. **Other income (loss)**

Code		
A	Other portfolio income (loss)	See the Partner's Instructions
B	Involuntary conversions	See the Partner's Instructions
C	Sec. 1256 contracts & straddles	Form 6781, line 1
D	Mining exploration costs recapture	See Pub. 535
E	Cancellation of debt	Form 1040, line 21 or Form 982
F	Other income (loss)	See the Partner's Instructions

12. **Section 179 deduction** — See the Partner's Instructions
13. **Other deductions**

Code		
A	Cash contributions (50%)	
B	Cash contributions (30%)	
C	Noncash contributions (50%)	
D	Noncash contributions (30%)	See the Partner's Instructions
E	Capital gain property to a 50% organization (30%)	
F	Capital gain property (20%)	
G	Contributions (100%)	
H	Investment interest expense	Form 4952, line 1
I	Deductions—royalty income	Schedule E, line 19
J	Section 59(e)(2) expenditures	See the Partner's Instructions
K	Deductions—portfolio (2% floor)	Schedule A, line 23
L	Deductions—portfolio (other)	Schedule A, line 28
M	Amounts paid for medical insurance	Schedule A, line 1 or Form 1040, line 29
N	Educational assistance benefits	See the Partner's Instructions
O	Dependent care benefits	Form 2441, line 12
P	Preproductive period expenses	See the Partner's Instructions
Q	Commercial revitalization deduction from rental real estate activities	See Form 8582 instructions
R	Pensions and IRAs	See the Partner's Instructions
S	Reforestation expense deduction	See the Partner's Instructions
T	Domestic production activities information	See Form 8903 instructions
U	Qualified production activities income	Form 8903, line 7b
V	Employer's Form W-2 wages	Form 8903, line 17
W	Other deductions	See the Partner's Instructions

14. **Self-employment earnings (loss)**

Note: If you have a section 179 deduction or any partner-level deductions, see the Partner's Instructions before completing Schedule SE.

A	Net earnings (loss) from self-employment	Schedule SE, Section A or B
B	Gross farming or fishing income	See the Partner's Instructions
C	Gross non-farm income	See the Partner's Instructions

15. **Credits**

A	Low-income housing credit (section 42(j)(5)) from pre-2008 buildings	
B	Low-income housing credit (other) from pre-2008 buildings	
C	Low-income housing credit (section 42(j)(5)) from post-2007 buildings	See the Partner's Instructions
D	Low-income housing credit (other) from post-2007 buildings	
E	Qualified rehabilitation expenditures (rental real estate)	
F	Other rental real estate credits	
G	Other rental credits	
H	Undistributed capital gains credit	Form 1040, line 73; check box a
I	Biofuel producer credit	
J	Work opportunity credit	See the Partner's Instructions
K	Disabled access credit	

Code		Report on
L	Empowerment zone employment credit	
M	Credit for increasing research activities	
N	Credit for employer social security and Medicare taxes	See the Partner's Instructions
O	Backup withholding	
P	Other credits	

16. **Foreign transactions**

A	Name of country or U.S. possession	
B	Gross income from all sources	Form 1116, Part I
C	Gross income sourced at partner level	

Foreign gross income sourced at partnership level

D	Passive category	
E	General category	Form 1116, Part I
F	Other	

Deductions allocated and apportioned at partner level

G	Interest expense	Form 1116, Part I
H	Other	Form 1116, Part I

Deductions allocated and apportioned at partnership level to foreign source income

I	Passive category	
J	General category	Form 1116, Part I
K	Other	

Other information

L	Total foreign taxes paid	Form 1116, Part II
M	Total foreign taxes accrued	Form 1116, Part II
N	Reduction in taxes available for credit	Form 1116, line 12
O	Foreign trading gross receipts	Form 8873
P	Extraterritorial income exclusion	Form 8873
Q	Other foreign transactions	See the Partner's Instructions

17. **Alternative minimum tax (AMT) items**

A	Post-1986 depreciation adjustment	
B	Adjusted gain or loss	See the Partner's
C	Depletion (other than oil & gas)	Instructions and
D	Oil, gas, & geothermal—gross income	the Instructions for
E	Oil, gas, & geothermal—deductions	Form 6251
F	Other AMT items	

18. **Tax-exempt income and nondeductible expenses**

A	Tax-exempt interest income	Form 1040, line 8b
B	Other tax-exempt income	See the Partner's Instructions
C	Nondeductible expenses	See the Partner's Instructions

19. **Distributions**

A	Cash and marketable securities	
B	Distribution subject to section 737	See the Partner's Instructions
C	Other property	

20. **Other information**

A	Investment income	Form 4952, line 4a
B	Investment expenses	Form 4952, line 5
D	Fuel tax credit information	Form 4136
E	Qualified rehabilitation expenditures (other than rental real estate)	See the Partner's Instructions
F	Basis of energy property	See the Partner's Instructions
G	Recapture of low-income housing credit (section 42(j)(5))	Form 8611, line 8
H	Recapture of low-income housing credit (other)	Form 8611, line 8
I	Recapture of investment credit	See Form 4255
J	Recapture of other credits	See the Partner's Instructions
K	Look-back interest—completed long-term contracts	See Form 8697
L	Look-back interest—income forecast method	See Form 8866
M	Dispositions of property with section 179 deductions	
N	Recapture of section 179 deduction	
O	Interest expense for corporate partners	
P	Section 453(l)(3) information	
Q	Section 453A(c) information	
R	Section 1260(b) information	See the Partner's
S	Interest allocable to production expenditures	instructions
T	CCF nonqualified withdrawals	
U	Depletion information—oil and gas	
V	Reserved	
W	Unrelated business taxable income	
X	Precontribution gain (loss)	
Y	Section 108(i) information	
Z	Net investment income	
	Other information	

INCOME TAX DEDUCTIONS

What Expenses Are Deductible?

Few of us ever test our powers of deduction, except when filling out an income tax form.
—Laurence J Peter

TRYING TO DETERMINE YOUR INCOME tax deductions at tax time can leave you full of questions about what kinds of expenses are deductible.

While doing bookkeeping and using income tax software, it is a really good idea to already know what these deductions are before tax time so that your chart of accounts can be set-up accordingly.

The income tax forms and tax deduction lists you find here will help answer many of your questions about what expenses are deductible. Keep in mind that starting in 2018, you will not be able to deduct out of pocket employee expenses at an itemized deduction on Schedule A, therefore these will only be relevant for those who receive a 1099-M.

I have included tax deduction lists for:

- Airline personnel
- Business professionals
- Day care providers
- Direct sellers
- Educators
- Firefighters
- Hairstylists
- Law enforcement
- Long Haul Truckers
- Realtors
- Vehicle, Travel & Entertainment

AIRLINE PERSONNEL

Airline personnel are able to deduct:

- uniforms
- laundry
- cockpit keys
- ear piece protectors
- flashlight/batteries
- flight bag
- professional fees
- mileage
- equipment expenses
- and more

AIRLINE PERSONNEL DEDUCTIONS

Client: _____ ID# _____ Tax Year _____

The purpose of this worksheet is to help you organize your tax deductible business expenses. In order for an expense to be deductible, it must be considered an "ordinary and necessary" expense. You may include other applicable expenses. Do not include expenses for which you have been reimbursed, expect to be reimbursed, or are reimbursable.

Uniforms
Alterations/Repairs	
Belts	
Emblems/Insignia/Wings	
Gloves	
Hat	
Jacket/Overcoat	
Laundry/Dry Cleaning	
Pants	
Shirts/Blouses	
Shoes/Boots	
Sweater/Vest	
Ties/Scarf	
Other -	
Other -	
Total	

Professional
Bidding/Software/Fees	
Books/Manuals/Tapes	
Business Cards	
Internet	
FAA Medical Exam	
ID Replacement	
Licenses	
Passport/Photo/Visa	
Professional Dues	
Subscriptions/Publications	
Training Expense	
Union Dues/Assessments	
Union Ofcr./Committee	
Other -	
Other -	
Total	

Mileage
Physicals	
Training	
Other -	
Total	

Vehicle & Travel
See Vehicle, Travel & Entertainment Worksheet

Equipment
Alarm Clock/Portable	
Calculators	
Cockpit Keys	
Ear Piece/Protectors	
Flashlight/Batteries	
Flight Bag	
Jet Bridge Keys	
Log Book	
Luggage/Garment Bag	
Maps/Charts	
Name Tags	
Portable Security Device	
Sunglasses	
Translators	
Voltage Converter	
Watch/Batteries	
Other -	
Other -	
Other -	
Total	

Telephone
Second Line	
Long Distance	
Pay Phone	
Cellular	
Answering Machine	
Fax Line	
Pager	
Other -	
Total	

Other Information
_____

Provided By: www.Bookkeeping-Basics.net

BUSINESS PROFESSIONALS

Business Professionals are able to deduct:

- business cards
- computer supplies
- dues & subscriptions
- gifts
- meals & entertainment
- ongoing education
- postage
- professional fees
- telephone/cell phone expenses
- travel
- equipment purchases
- other miscellaneous expenses

BUSINESS PROFESSIONALS DEDUCTIONS

Client: _____ ID# _____ Tax Year _____

Miscellaneous	
Business Cards	
Clerical	
Computer Supplies	
Customer Lists	
Gifts	
Office Supplies	
Postage	
Photocopying	
Printing	
Repairs	
Shipping	
Stationery	
Other -	
Other -	
Total	

The purpose of this worksheet is to help you organize your tax deductible business expenses. In order for an expense to be deductible, it must be considered an "ordinary and necessary" expense. You may include other applicable expenses. Do not include expenses for which you have been reimbursed, expect to be reimbursed, or are reimbursable.

Telephone	
Long Distance	
Faxes	
Pay Phone	
Cellular	
2nd Line	
Beeper/Pager	
Answering Service	
Other -	
Other -	
Total	

Professional	
Dues	
E & O Insurance	
Legal & Professional	
Licenses	
Memberships	
Publications	
Seminars	
Continuing Education	
Resumes	
Other -	
Other -	
Other -	
Other -	
Other -	
Other -	
Total	

Equipment	
Attache Case	
Calculator	
Camera	
Desk	
Chair	
Filing Cabinet	
Cell Phone	
Software	
Tape Recorder	
Telephone	
Other -	
Other -	
Total	

Vehicle & Travel
See Vehicle, Travel & Entertainment Worksheet

Other Information

Provided By: **www.Bookkeeping-Basics.net**

DAY CARE PROVIDERS

Day Care Providers are able to deduct:

- books & magazines
- car seats
- child proofing
- continuing education
- CPR training
- furniture
- insurance
- ordinary supplies
- vehicle & travel
- playground equipment
- business use of home
- and more

DAY CARE PROVIDER

Client: _____ ID# _____ Tax Year _____

The purpose of this worksheet is to help you organize your tax deductible business expenses. In order for an expense to be deductible, it must be considered an "ordinary and necessary" expense. You may include other applicable expenses. Do not include expenses for which you have been reimbursed, expect to be reimbursed, or are reimbursable.

Ordinary Supplies	
Advertising	
Books & Magazines	
Business Tax	
Child Proofing Devices	
Continuing Education	
CPR Training	
Food & Snacks	
Insurance: Bond	
Insurance: Business	
Insurance: Liability	
License & Permits	
Payroll: Wages	
Payroll: Taxes	
Professional Fees: Legal	
Professional Fees: Tax Prep	
Repairs	
Replacements	
Supplies: Art	
Supplies: Bottles, Diapers, etc.	
Supplies: Cleaning	
Supplies: Household	
Supplies: Laundry	
Supplies: Office	
Supplies: Party	
Telephone: cell	
Telephone: House	
Telephone: Pager	
Tickets, Fees, Field Trips, etc.	
Toys	
Video Rentals	
Other -	
Other -	
Total	

Vehicle & Travel
See Vehicle, Travel & Ent. Worksheet

Other Information

Major Purchases	
Car Seats	
Cribs	
High Chairs	
Riding Equipment	
Swing Set/Slides	
Other -	
Other -	
Purchases (Subject to % of business use)	
Computer Equipment	
Dishwasher	
Dryer	
Fencing	
Refrigerator	
Television	
VCR	
Washer	
Other -	
Other -	
Total	

Business Use of Home	
Total Square Feet of Home	
Business Area of Home	
Business Hours (Yearly)	
Home Mortgage Interest	
Property Taxes	
Insurance	
Rents	
Allocated Expenses (subject to % of business use)	
Cleaning Service	
Gardner	
Maintenance & Repairs	
Pool Service & Supplies	
Repairs	
Utilities: Cable	
Utilities: Gas & Electric	
Utilities: Trash	
Utilities: Water	
Other -	
Other -	
Total	

Provided By: **www.Bookkeeping-Basics.net**

DIRECT SELLERS

Direct Sellers are able to deduct the following:

- advertising
- dues & subscriptions
- insurance
- inventory
- materials & supplies
- sales expenses
- professional fees
- postage
- telephone expenses
- travel & mileage
- equipment purchases
- and more

DIRECT SELLER DEDUCTIONS

Client: _____   ID# _____   Tax Year _____

The purpose of this worksheet is to help you organize your tax deductible business expenses. In order for an expense to be deductible, it must be considered an "ordinary and necessary" expense. You may include other applicable expenses. Do not include expenses for which you have been reimbursed, expect to be reimbursed, or are reimbursable.

Inventory

Inventory at Beginning of Yr	
Purchases	
Cost of Items Personal Use	
Other Costs	
Inventory at End of Year	

Sales Expenses

Advertising	
Business Cards	
Bank Charges	
Catalogues	
Commissions	
Demos	
Freight	
Gifts	
Kits	
Map Books	
Postage	
Refunds	
Sales Aids	
Sales Assistants	
Samples & Promotional Items	
Seminars & Trade Shows	
Service Charges	
Snacks & Beverages	
Storage Containers	
Storage Fees	
Supplies - Meeting/Party	
Supplies - Miscellaneous	
Supplies - Office	
Other -	
Total	

Vehicle & Travel

See Vehicle, Travel & Entertainment Worksheet	

Professional

Dues	
Insurance	
License	
Publications	
Other -	
Other -	
Total	

Telephone

Long Distance	
Faxes	
Pay Phone	
Cellular	
2nd Line	
Beeper/Pager	
Answering Service	
Other -	
Other -	
Telephone	
Total	

Equipment

Attache Case	
Calculator	
Desk	
Display Tables	
Camera	
Filing Cabinet	
Cell Phone	
Telephone	
Other -	
Other -	
Total	

Other Information

_____
_____

Provided By: www.Bookkeeping-Basics.net

EDUCATORS

Educators are able to deduct the following:

- classroom aid expenses
- furniture
- membership dues
- ongoing education
- professional fees
- party supplies
- prizes and awards
- telephone
- tools
- equipment
- uniform
- other miscellaneous

EDUCATOR DEDUCTIONS

Client: _____ ID# _____ Tax Year _____

The purpose of this worksheet is to help you organize your tax deductible business expenses. In order for an expense to be deductible, it must be considered an "ordinary and necessary" expense. You may include other applicable expenses. Do not include expenses for which you have been reimbursed, expect to be reimbursed, or are reimbursable.

Classroom Aids

Attendance Books	
Arts & Crafts	
Audio Visual	
Books	
Decorations	
Food	
Grade Books	
Rentals	
Software	
Film/Processing	
Photocopying	
Printing	
Publications	
Party Supplies	
Tools	
Trophies	
Prizes & Awards	
Stationary	
Other -	
Other -	
Total	

Professional

Conventions	
Dues	
E & O Insurance	
Job Seeking	
Legal Fees	
Licenses	
Memberships	
Seminars	
Continuing Ed	
Resumes	
School Functions	
Other -	
Other -	
Total	

Vehicle & Travel

See Vehicle, Travel & Entertainment Worksheet

Telephone

Long Distance	
Faxes	
Pay Phone	
Cellular	
2nd Line	
Beeper/Pager	
Answering Service	
Other -	
Other -	
Total	

Equipment

Calculator	
Camera	
Desk	
Chair	
Filing Cabinet	
Cell Phone	
Tape Recorder	
Other -	
Other -	
Other -	
Total	

Uniforms

Dry Cleaning	
Laundry	
Lab Coats	
Other -	
Total	

Miscellaneous

Postage	
Storage	
Other -	
Total	

Other Information

_____

Provided By: www.Bookkeeping-Basics.net

FIREFIGHTERS

Firefighters are able to deduct the following:

- uniforms
- boots
- emblems
- professional fees
- continuing education
- equipment
- meals
- union dues
- subscriptions
- travel & entertainment
- and more

FIREFIGHTER DEDUCTIONS

Client: _____ ID# _____ Tax Year _____

Uniforms

Uniforms	
Belts	
Boots, Shoes	
Gloves	
Hat, Helmet	
Jacket	
Pants	
Shirts	
Ties	
Emblems, Insignia	
Dry Cleaning	
Laundry	
Other -	
Other -	
Total	

The purpose of this worksheet is to help you organize your tax deductible business expenses. In order for an expense to be deductible, it must be considered an "ordinary and necessary" expense. You may include other applicable expenses. Do not include expenses for which you have been reimbursed, expect to be reimbursed, or are reimbursable.

Vehicle & Travel

See Vehicle, Travel & Entertainment Worksheet

Equipment

Badges, Name Tags	
Briefcase	
Binoculars	
Flashlight, bulbs, batteries	
Maps	
Notebook	
Pager, Beeper	
Equipment Repairs	
Safety Equipment	
Tape Recorder	
Tapes	
Other -	
Other -	
Total	

Professional

Union Dues	
Association Dues	
Professional Dues	
Subscriptions	
Other -	
Other -	
Total	

Continuing Education

Union Dues	
Association Dues	
Professional Dues	
Subscriptions	
Other -	
Other -	
Total	

Insurance

Errors & Omissions	
Other -	
Other -	
Total	

Meals

House Dues	
Business Meals on-the-job	
Other -	
Other -	
Total	

Telephone

2nd Line	
Long Distance	
Pay Phone	
Cellular	
Answering Machine	
Fax Line	
Other -	
Total	

Other Information

_____

_____

Provided By: www.Bookkeeping-Basics.net

HAIRSTYLIST/MANICURISTS

Hairstylist and Manicurists are able to deduct:
- dues & subscriptions
- professional fees
- telephone expenses
- ongoing education
- laundry
- client gifts
- rent
- refreshments for customers
- scissors
- linens & supplies
- travel
- other miscellaneous expenses

HAIRSTYLIST/MANICURIST DEDUCTIONS

Client: _____ ID# _____ Tax Year _____

The purpose of this worksheet is to help you organize your tax deductible business expenses. In order for an expense to be deductible, it must be considered an "ordinary and necessary" expense. You may include other applicable expenses. Do not include expenses for which you have been reimbursed, expect to be reimbursed, or are reimbursable.

Miscellaneous

Business Cards	
Public Relations/Photos	
Refreshments for Customers	
Client Gifts	
Office Supplies	
Postage	
Rent	
Assistant Fees	
Shampoo Person Expenses	
Laundry	
Cleaning Expense	
Other -	
Other -	
Total	

Professional

Dues & Professional Fees	
Liability Insurance	
Legal & Professional	
Licenses	
Business Tax	
Memberships	
Publications	
Hair Shows	
Seminars	
Other -	
Other -	
Total	

Telephone

Telephone	
Answering Service	
Pager/Voice Mail	
Cellular Phone	
Pay Phone	
Long Distance	
Other -	
Other -	
Total	

Equipment & Supplies

Hairdryers, Drills, Etc.	
Hair Products	
Nail Products	
Miscellaneous Supplies	
Telephone	
Cellular Phone	
Pager	
Equipment Repairs	
Equipment Rental	
Other -	
Other -	
Total	

Vehicle & Travel

See Vehicle, Travel & Ent. Worksheet

Other Information

_____
_____
_____
_____

Provided By: www.Bookkeeping-Basics.net

LAW ENFORCEMENT OFFICERS

Law Enforcement officers are able to deduct:

- ammo pouch
- bullet proof vest
- ear protectors
- emblems
- uniforms
- professional fees
- insurance
- equipment & supplies
- telephone
- travel expenses
- whistle
- and more

LAW ENFORCEMENT DEDUCTIONS

Client: _____   ID# _____   Tax Year _____

The purpose of this worksheet is to help you organize your tax deductible business expenses. In order for an expense to be deductible, it must be considered an "ordinary and necessary" expense. You may include other applicable expenses. Do not include expenses for which you have been reimbursed, expect to be reimbursed, or are reimbursable.

Uniforms

Uniforms	
Belts	
Boots, Shoes	
Gloves	
Hat, Helmet	
Jacket	
Pants	
Shirts	
Ties	
Emblems, Insignia	
Dry Cleaning	
Laundry	
Rain Gear	
Other -	
Other -	
Total	

Professional

Registration	
Fingerprinting	
Licenses & Permits	
Union Dues	
Association Dues	
Professional Dues	
Range Dues	
Subscriptions	
Textbooks	
Seminars	
Workshops	
Books, Manuals	
Supplies	
Other -	
Other -	
Total	

Insurance

Bond	
Errors & Omissions	
Other -	
Other -	
Total	

Vehicle & Travel

See Vehicle, Travel & Entertainment Worksheet

Equipment/Supplies

Ammo Pouch	
Ammunition	
Badges, Name Tags	
Baton	
Briefcase	
Bulletproof Vest	
Ear Protectors	
Camera	
Film & Processing	
Flashlight, Bulbs, Batteries	
Guns	
Mace	
Maps	
Notebook	
Pager, Beeper	
Equipment Repairs	
Safety Equipment	
Tape Recorder	
Tapes	
Whistle	
Other -	
Other -	
Total	

Telephone

2nd Line	
Long Distance	
Pay Phone	
Cellular	
Answering Machine	
Fax Line	
Other -	
Other -	
Total	

Provided By: www.Bookkeeping-Basics.net

LONG HAUL TRUCKERS

Long Haul and Overnight Drivers can deduct:

- baggage/luggage and shipping
- bath/shower
- laundry
- locker fees
- out of town travel expenses
- owner operator truck expenses
- parking & tolls
- dues & fees
- supplies
- toiletries
- other miscellaneous expenses

LONG HAUL TRUCKER/OVERNIGHT DRIVER

Client: _____ ID# _____ Tax Year _____

Out of Town Travel Expenses	
Baggage & Shipping	
Bath/Shower	
Car Rental & Gas	
Laundry/Laundry Supplies	
Locker Fees	
Lodging	
Meals (Actual Cost)	
Parking & Tolls	
Taxi, Bus, Shuttles	
Telephone/Fax	
Tips	
Toiletries	
Transportation, Air Fare	
Other -	
Total	

The purpose of this worksheet is to help you organize your tax deductible business expenses. In order for an expense to be deductible, it must be considered an "ordinary and necessary" expense. You may include other applicable expenses. Do not include expenses for which you have been reimbursed, expect to be reimbursed, or are reimbursable.

Miscellaneous Expenses	
Business Cards & Stationary	
Delivery Expenses - Postage	
Insurance - Business	
Legal & Professional Fees	
Office Supplies	
Safety Classes	
Secretarial Services	
Testing - Job Related	
Total	

Owner Operator Truck Expenses	
Description of Truck	
Date Placed in Service	
Odometer - Beginning of Yr	
Odometer - End of Year	
Interest Paid	
Gas, Lube, Oil	
Repairs & Maintenance	
Tires	
Insurance	
License/Registration Fee	
Other -	
Total	

Supplies	
Back Supporter	
Batteries	
Cellular Phone	
Citizens Band Radio	
Compass/GPS	
Fire Extinguisher	
First Aid Kit	
Flares	
Flashlight	
Glasses - Safety & Sun	
Gloves	
Ice Chest/Thermos	
Map/Map Book	
Radio	
Safety Boots/Shoes	
Seat Cushion	
Tools	
Trade Publications	
Uniforms & Maintenance	
Weather Receiver	
Other -	
Total	

Dues & Fees	
License	
Permits/Fees	
Security Bond	
Trade Association Dues	
Travel Card Fees	
Union Dues	
Other -	
Total	

Other Information

_____

_____

Provided By: www.Bookkeeping-Basics.net

REALTORS

Realtors are able to deduct the following:

- advertising
- business cards
- bank charges
- client gifts
- commissions
- flowers/cards
- ongoing education
- sales expenses
- professional fees
- telephone
- travel expenses
- and more

REALTOR DEDUCTIONS

Client: _____   ID# _____   Tax Year _____

The purpose of this worksheet is to help you organize your tax deductible business expenses. In order for an expense to be deductible, it must be considered an "ordinary and necessary" expense. You may include other applicable expenses. Do not include expenses for which you have been reimbursed, expect to be reimbursed, or are reimbursable.

Sales

Advertising	
Appraisal Fees	
Business Cards	
Bank Charges	
Clerical	
Client Gifts	
Courier Service	
Commissions Paid	
Escrow/Loan Fees	
Referral Fees	
Film/Processing	
Flowers/Cards	
Keys/Locksmith	
Lock Boxes	
Map Books	
Office Expense	
Open House	
Rent	
Sales Assistants	
Repairs	
Signs, Flags, Banners	
Food	
Software	
Photocopying	
Printing	
Tools	
Stationery	
Other -	
Other -	
Total	

Professional

Dues	
Errors & Omissions	
Legal Fees	
Licenses	
Memberships	
Multiple Listing	
Publications	
Total	

Professional

Seminars	
Continuing Education	
Resumes	
Other -	
Other -	
Total	

Telephone

Long Distance	
Faxes	
Pay Phone	
Cellular	
2nd Line	
Beeper/Pager	
Answering Service	
Other -	
Other -	
Total	

Equipment

Attache Case	
Calculator	
Desk	
Camera	
Chair	
Filing Cabinet	
Cell Phone	
Tape Recorder	
Other -	
Other -	
Total	

Vehicle & Travel

See Vehicle, Travel & Entertainment Worksheet

Provided By: www.Bookkeeping-Basics.net

VEHICLE, TRAVEL & ENTERTAINMENT

Many different professions can deduct vehicle mileage, travel and entertainment expenses. Following are some of the things you will need to track in order to claim these deductions:

- date vehicle placed in service
- beginning and ending odometer readings
- total miles driven in the year
- total business miles driven in the year
- total commute miles
- parking & tolls
- property tax
- meal receipts with name of client
- and more

VEHICLE, TRAVEL ENTERTAINMENT EXPENSES

Client: _____ ID# _____ Tax Year _____

The purpose of this worksheet is to help you organize your tax deductible business expenses. In order for an expense to be deductible, it must be considered an "ordinary and necessary" expense. You may include other applicable expenses. Do not include expenses for which you have been reimbursed, expect to be reimbursed, or are reimbursable.

Vehicle Expense	
Description of vehicle	
Date placed in service	
Odometer reading beginning of year	
Odometer reading end of year	
Total Miles	
Business Miles	
Commute Miles	
Daily Average round-trip commute	
Personal Miles	
Is car leased?	
Is car owned? (or financed)?	
Was this vehicle depreciated in a prior year?	
Gas, Lube, Oil	
Repairs & Maintenance	
Tires	
Towing	
Insurance	
Auto License/Registration	
Personal Property Tax	
Lease Payments	
Interest	
Auto Club	

Vehicle Expense	
Warranty	
Smog Certificate	
Other -	
Other -	
Total	

Travel & Entertainment Expense	
Airfare, Train	
Car rental & gas	
Parking, Tolls	
Taxi, Bus, Shuttles	
Lodging	
Meals	
Entertainment	
Tips	
Telephone	
Dry Cleaning	
Number of days out of town	
Other -	
Other -	
Total	

Other Information

_____
_____

Provided By: www.Bookkeeping-Basics.net

ESTIMATED TAX PAYMENTS

Should You Adjust Your Quarterly Vouchers?

*We must adjust to changing times
and still hold to unchanging principles.
—Jimmy Carter*

SHOULD YOU ADJUST YOUR ESTIMATED tax payment if business is suddenly more or less than usual? The slowing down of the economy has affected businesses in all industries, from service to retail, causing many companies to re-evaluate their financial and tax situation.

If business is slower than normal, you may want to consider adjusting your quarterly estimated tax payment vouchers.

If you have made quarterly tax payments during the year, a change in your business's income, income tax deductions, credits and exemptions may make it necessary to re-figure your existing payments for the remainder of the year.

To avoid either a penalty from the IRS or overpaying the IRS interest-free, consider increasing or decreasing the amount of your remaining estimated payments.

CORPORATIONS

For calendar year corporations, estimated tax installments are due on April 15, June 15, September 15, and December 15. If any due date falls on a Saturday, Sunday or legal holiday, the payment is due on the first following business day.

To avoid a penalty, each installment must equal at least 25 percent of the lesser of:

100 percent of the tax shown on the current year's tax return (or of the actual tax, if no return is filed), or 100 percent of the income tax shown on the corporation's return for the preceding tax year, provided a positive tax liability was shown and the preceding tax year consisted of 12 months.

A lower installment amount may be paid if it is shown that use of an annualized income method, or for corporations with seasonal incomes, an adjusted seasonal method, would result in a lower required installment payment.

INDIVIDUALS

For individuals (including self-employed sole proprietors and partners), similar rules apply, with due dates on April 15, June 15, September 15, and January 15.

Individuals who do not pay at least 90 percent of their tax through withholding generally are required to estimate their income tax liability and make equal quarterly payments of the required annual payment liability during the year.

The required annual payment is the lesser of: 90 percent of the tax ultimately shown on the return for the tax year, or 90 percent of the tax due for the year if no return is filed.

100 percent of the tax shown on the taxpayer's return for the preceding year if that year was not for a short period of less than 12 months; or the annualized income installment.

For high-income taxpayers whose adjusted gross income (AGI) shown on the preceding year's tax return exceeds $150,000 (or $75,000 for a married individual filing separately).

The required annual payment is the lessor of 90 percent of the tax for the current year, or 110 percent of the tax shown on the income tax return for the preceding tax year.

PAYMENT VOUCHERS

If you expect an uneven income stream for the remainder of the year, or changes in the amount of income tax deductions, credits, exemptions, and other adjustments, your required estimated payments may not be the same for each remaining period, requiring adjustment to your tax payments.

The need for, and the extent of, adjustments to your estimated payments should be assessed at the end of each installment payment period.

If you discover within a payment period that a change in your business's anticipated income, deductions, credits, exemptions, or other taxes will either increase or decrease your tax liability, (and therefore the required annual payment expected for the rest of the year), you should adjust your remaining quarterly payments accordingly.

THE NO REFUND POLICY

Do you have a drop in income? Unfortunately, if your business has experienced a drop in income (and thus the installment payments you've already made were not necessary), the IRS will not provide you a quick refund of any payments already made.

You will have to wait until you file your federal income tax return for the tax year to apply any unnecessary tax payment installments against your final tax bill and seek a refund.

ADJUSTING TAX PAYMENTS

To change or amend your estimated tax payments, refigure your total estimated payments due. Then, figure the payment due for each remaining payment period.

However, be careful. If a tax payment for a previous period is less than one-fourth of your amended estimated tax, you may be subject to a penalty when you file your income tax return.

ACCOUNTING AND TAX SOFTWARE

Help With Online Preparation

Spectacular achievement is always preceded by unspectacular preparation.
—Robert H Schuller

ORGANIZING YOUR BUSINESS FINANCES is quick and easy with QuickBooks software. You can get quick access to everyday task like invoicing, bill tracking, check-writing and payroll.

As well as track sales and expenses, share your data with Microsoft Excel and your accountant, and save time completing routine tasks and paperwork enabling you to spend more time on your business.

QUICKBOOKS PREMIER

There are several different QuickBooks accounting software programs available. The main software that I recommend for bookkeepers is the QuickBooks Premier Accountant Edition.

QuickBooks Premier has all of the great features you know and love in QuickBooks Pro, plus industry-specific, time saving, ready-to-use reports and business planning tools tailored to help your company grow.

Along with saving you time on routine accounting tasks, Premier makes it simple to monitor business performance, build forecasts and manage payables and receivables. Premier also includes tools for tracking inventory, creating purchase orders and setting pricing levels.

QUICKBOOKS PRO

If you are using QuickBooks for your own personal use or for tracking rental real estate transactions, then I would recommend QuickBooks Pro for your bookkeeping needs.

It is the easiest way to track sales and expenses. All your finance information is organized in one place, so you can easily stay on top of your transactions and be ready for tax time.

QUICKBOOKS ONLINE

For businesses that need access to the books from multiple places and/or have multiple users in different locations, I recommend QuickBooks Online Essentials. It offers the essential accounting tools necessary to manage your business and the freedom to access your financial information from work, home, or the road.

QUICKBOOKS POINT OF SALE

You can rely on QuickBooks Point of Sale for easy access to the information that matters the most as you will have everything you need to make better daily business decisions.

The setup is really easy. You will be up and selling in about one day. Just use the simple setup interview to get started, then import existing customers, items or vendors lists from QuickBooks or MS Excel.

Easily accept credit cards, manage inventory, and track customers by collecting customer information as you ring up sales so you can see every purchase and return. Plus, with the built-in loyalty program, you can easily reward your best customers and keep them coming back for more.

QUICKBOOKS ACCOUNTING SOFTWARE

QuickBooks software makes bookkeeping and accounting easy with tools to organize your finances all in one place. It will help you to complete tasks like payroll, invoicing, bill tracking and check writing.

You can track sales and expenses, and easily share this data with MS Word and Excel. With QuickBooks bookkeeping forms and software, you will spend far less time on routine tasks and more time on business.

I have partnered with QuickBooks to be able to present to my clients and website visitors exclusive QB bookkeeping deals only offered from authorized QuickBooks affiliates. You can access these deals through my website at bookkeeping-basics.net/quickbooks/accounting-software.html.

ONLINE INCOME TAXES

There are many great options to choose from such as the following online income tax software:

- TurboTax Premier
- TurboTax Home and Business
- H&R Block Deluxe

- H&R Block Business

TURBOTAX PREMIER

This one includes everything that is in the standard version. TurboTax Premier Online Edition helps you make the most of your investments and rental property deductions.

Choose Turbo Tax Premier Online Edition for: Claiming stocks, bonds and mutual funds; Rental property guidance; Reporting of capital gains and losses; Help if you're the beneficiary of an estate or trust.

NEW! Audit Risk Alert tells you which claims may trigger an audit

TURBOTAX HOME AND BUSINESS

Tailored to your individual situation, TurboTax Home and Business will search for deductions and credits that might benefit you.

Choose TurboTax Home and Business for: Personal budgets, sole proprietor, partnerships and corporations.

H&R BLOCK DELUXE

Complex filing is made easy with H&R Block™ Deluxe. H&R Block Deluxe helps maximize your deductions.

Choose H&R Block Deluxe Edition for: Great for homeowners and investors; Maximizing mortgage interest and real estate taxes; Investment income and stock options.

NOW H&R Block Deduction Pro® is integrated to optimize your charitable donations.

H&R BLOCK BUSINESS

The premium business edition is great for small business owners.

Choose H&R Block Business for: Corporation or S-corporation, partnership and LLC, estates and trusts, non-profit returns, payroll and employer forms

INCOME TAX PROFESSIONALS

Are You At Risk?

The foundation stones for a balanced success are honesty, character, integrity, faith, love and loyalty.
—*Zig Ziglar*

RECENT IRS REPORTS HAVE highlighted the need for honest tax professionals because many tax experts are leaving their clients at risk of serious penalties. Is your current tax professional putting you at risk? Like most taxpayers, you probably want to receive a larger refund.

You should be aware of every tax deduction that you can legally take advantage of on your income tax filing in order to do so. However, some people either unknowingly or intentionally try to take advantage of income tax deductions that they shouldn't be receiving.

This can get them into major trouble with their taxes. A recent report from the IRS shows that many people are illegally taking advantage of tax credits that they shouldn't be receiving.

While many of these people aren't knowingly doing anything wrong, they risk massive penalties or possible criminal charges and may end up needing income tax resolutions help due to the actions of unscrupulous tax professionals.

This report clearly demonstrates the need for honest tax professionals. The IRS states that many people aren't trying to actually break the law.

Some dishonest tax preparers are actually illegally misrepresenting their clients' income, which means unsuspecting clients can face serious consequences down the road.

You should speak with a legitimate tax expert ensure you aren't violating any laws.

Are you or your tax professional making any of these mistakes, or do you have a need for honest tax professional help?

WARNING

The IRS recently warned people about a recent scheme that many dishonest tax preparers are using. They will over report their client's income to help them receive a larger tax return.

How can this possibly work? Aren't you supposed to pay higher taxes if you have a higher income? Not necessarily.

There is a loophole in the tax code that dishonest tax preparers are illegally taking trying to exploit, which could be leaving their clients at risk.

This new scam works by taking advantage of the Earned Income Tax Credit, which is a provision created in 1975 to reduce hardships for low to moderate income families by lowering the tax owed to the IRS.

There is a need for honest Santa Rosa tax professionals as many people may receive tax returns for money that they earned, even if they didn't pay taxes during the year.

TAX CALCULATOR

According to the Intuit Tax Calculator, a couple of two earning $20,304 or less wouldn't have to pay any taxes in 2014. However, they would still be eligible for a tax credit.

The IRS tax tool shows that if a couple reported that their income was $20,304 (enough to not have to pay a cent to the IRS), then they would receive a tax refund of $12.

If they reported that their income was $15,000 then they would receive $417. The credit would be much higher if they had children.

The catch is that you can only receive the earned income tax credit if your income is over $13,650. If your income is below that limit, then you still won't have to pay taxes to the IRS, but you won't receive a generous refund.

TAX REPORTING

The IRS recently reported that some dishonest tax companies are illegally over reporting clients' earnings to help them receive a credit that they are not eligible for.

These agents are often compensated a percentage of their client's tax refund, so they have an incentive to lie to help you get a larger return.

Why should you be concerned if your accountant is helping you receive a larger refund? Because *you* are the one that the IRS will come after if they find out. The IRS plans to start cracking down on this problem, because some experts estimate that the fraud rate is about 25%, which is a serious cause for concern.

You will need to be sure to hire an honest tax preparer to avoid these consequences.

HIRING

At Horne Financial Services we are committed to helping you receive every cent that you deserve. However, we also want to make sure that your taxes are honestly reported so that you don't get in trouble if you are audited by the IRS. Please don't hesitate to contact us if you are in need of an honest tax expert. We look forward to helping you receive the refund that you deserve!

TAX SERVICES

Military & Public Service Members

Earn your success based on service to others, not at the expense of others.
—H Jackson Brown Jr

DID YOU KNOW THAT MAY IS national military appreciation month? There are many different tax benefits that are available to members of the military and their families.

Each year, there is a free booklet produced that is packed with valuable information and tips designed to help service members and their families take advantage of all tax benefits allowed by law.

MILITARY SERVICES

Reservists whose reserve-related duties take them more than 100 miles from home can deduct their un-reimbursed travel expenses on Form 2106 or Form 2106-E-Z, even if they don't itemize their income tax deductions.

Eligible un-reimbursed moving expenses are deductible expenses on Form 3903.

Low-and moderate-income service members often qualify for such family-friendly tax benefits as the Earned Income Tax Credit, and a special computation method is available for those who receive combat pay.

Low-and moderate-income service members who contribute to an IRA or 401(k)-type retirement plan, such as the federal government's Thrift Savings Plan, can often claim the saver's credit, also known as the retirement plan savings contributions credit, on Form 8880.

COMBAT PAY

Service members stationed abroad have extra time, until June 15, to file a federal income tax return. Those serving in a combat zone have even longer, typically until 180 days after they leave the combat zone.

Service members may qualify to delay payment of income tax due before or during their period of service. See Publication 3 for details including how to request tax relief.

Service members who prepare their own return qualify to electronically file their federal return for free using IRS free online income taxes file.

In addition, the IRS partners with the military through the Volunteer Income Tax Assistance program to provide free tax preparation to service members and their families at bases in the United States and around the world.

TAX PREP SUMMARY

If you know of any Military or public service members needing help with getting the most out of the income tax deductions available to them, please let them know it would be an honor to help them.

At Horne Financial Services we specialize in tax preparation and bookkeeping services for military and other public service members.

INCOME TAX RESOLUTION

Help Clear Up Disputes, Penalties And Back Taxes

Character is the ability to carry out a good resolution long after the excitement of the moment has passed.
—Cavett Robert

DO YOU KNOW WHAT TO DO if there is an issue with your tax return? Get income tax resolution help with clearing up your disputes, penalties, interest and back taxes that are owed.

It can be very scary and stressful when you are

experiencing income tax filing liability issues and don't know where to go or what to do to help resolve the problem.

However, there is help available to help you through the process of clearing everything up in the quickest, easiest, most cost efficient and stress free manner possible. Following are some of the tax resolution issues you may need help with.

- Audits
- Dispute Tax Return Changes
- Reduce Penalties and Interest
- Back Taxes
- Remove Levy or Tax Lien
- Non Filed Tax Returns
- Income Tax Preparation
- Amendments
- Offer In Compromise
- Installment Agreement

There are a few different options for helping to resolve the issue depending upon which one you are dealing with.

For example, you may want help with filling out and filing an offer in compromise which can help you to greatly reduce any outstanding liability.

Or, you could possibly use some help with filling out and filing an innocent spouse form when you need to disassociate yourself with an ex spouse's tax liability that doesn't belong to you. You will learn more about both of these options in the next chapter.

TAX SOLUTIONS

As an Enrolled Agent, I am ready and able to help with your tax resolution case for both Federal and State tax issues in ALL states.

We will work together to fight for your taxpayer rights no matter how much is owed to help get rid of as much of the tax debt as possible in a fast and efficient manner.

INCOME TAX FORMS

Following are three helpful forms that are often used in the tax resolution process:

- Power of Attorney (Form 2848)
- Offer In Compromise (Form 656)
- Innocent Spouse Relief (Form 8857)

INCOME TAX CONSULTATION

Call now at (707) 795-1320 or use my simple online scheduling system at schedulicity.com/scheduling/HFSFVD to set up a free initial consultation to speak with me directly about your Federal or State tax debt concerns.

Or, fill in the tax resolution estimate form at bookkeeping-basics.net/tax-resolution.html to get a free estimate and book an appointment via phone or email.

We will determine what kind of forms will need to be filed and come up with a schedule of payments for income tax resolution services that will fit your budget.

Make sure to ask about the discount when paying in lump sum.

I appreciate the opportunity to help you start to get rid of that tax problem today!

TAX RELIEF

Help Lower Tax Liabilities

We want to deliver tax relief all across the country, no matter where you live.
—Kevin Brady

THERE IS ADDITIONAL TAX RELIEF available to help lower your tax liabilities. Find out how to obtain tax help through Military Relief, Innocent Spouse Relief, Disaster and Emergency Assistance Relief and more.

After Congress successfully got through a one year patch and reached the serious consideration stage, the now annual tax extenders packages are poised waiting for the right moment to jump onto the legislative bandwagon

Read about some of the most common forms of tax extender relief options available below.

MILITARY TAX RELIEF

The Heroes Earnings Assistance and Relief Tax Act (HEART) was supposed to provide more than $1.2 billion in tax benefits to members of the military who are receiving combat pay, saving for retirement plans or purchasing homes.

The bill eased certain rules in order to allow military families to qualify for the earned income tax credit (EITC), make penalty-free withdrawals from pension plans and access amounts in health flexible spending arrangements.

The bill was supposed to also enable thousands of active-duty military families to qualify for the economic stimulus payments, even when a spouse does not have a Social Security number.

Under prior law, some families were denied stimulus payments because one spouse was an immigrant and did not have a Social Security number.

DISASTER ASSISTANCE AND EMERGENCY RELIEF

Special tax law provisions may help taxpayers and businesses recover financially from the impact of a disaster, especially when the federal government declares their location to be a major disaster area.

Depending on the circumstances, the IRS may grant additional time to file returns and pay taxes. Both individuals and businesses in a federally declared disaster area can get a faster refund by claiming losses related to the disaster on the tax return for the previous year, usually by filing an amended return for tax relief.

The IRS also offers audio presentations on Planning for Disaster. These presentations discuss business planning, insurance coverage, record keeping and other tips to stay in business after a major disaster.

INNOCENT SPOUSE RELIEF

There are several income tax resolution options available to help eliminate your tax burden. By requesting innocent spouse relief, you can be relieved of responsibility for paying tax, interest, and penalties if your spouse (or former spouse) improperly reported items or omitted items on your tax return.

Generally, the tax, interest, and penalties that qualify for relief can only be collected from your spouse (or former spouse).

However, you are jointly and individually responsible for any tax, interest, and penalties that do not qualify for relief. The IRS can collect these amounts from either you or your spouse (or former spouse).

You must meet all of the following conditions to qualify for innocent spouse relief:

1. You filed a joint return.
2. There is an understated tax on the return that is due to erroneous items (defined later) of your spouse (or former spouse).

3. You can show that when you signed the joint return you did not know, and had no reason to know, that the understated tax existed (or the extent to which the understated tax existed).
4. Taking into account all the facts and circumstances, it would be unfair to hold you liable for the understated tax.

Innocent spouse relief will not be granted if the IRS proves that you and your spouse (or former spouse) transferred property to one another as part of a fraudulent scheme.

A fraudulent scheme includes a scheme to defraud the IRS or another third party, such as a creditor, former spouse, or business partner.

TAX ORGANIZER

Get Prepared For Filing Taxes

The more we can organize, find and manage information, the more effectively we can function in our modern world.
—Vint Cerf

TAX ORGANIZERS CAN HELP by facilitating the process of pulling together your tax information. A basic organizer such as what is shown here is designed for new clients and allows you to enter your information right on the screen or you can print and fill out by hand.

If you use the online version, you can print the completed organizer and fax, mail or hand deliver it to the office. Existing clients should be able to call the office and request a pro-forma organizer that includes prior year information and carryover data.

GENERAL TAX ORGANIZER

Whenever you are filling out an organizer, make sure to fill in the form completely so that your preparer knows that you didn't accidentally forget anything. The tax organizer includes the following categories:

Tax Organizer Main Information Sheet

Name, address, SS#, dependent info, birthdate, and phone number.

GENERAL INFORMATION

2017 (MAIN INFO)

Taxpayer's First Name _____ M.I. _____ Spouse's First Name _____ Spouse's M.I. _____

Taxpayer's Last Name _____ Suffix _____ Spouse's Last Name (if different) _____

Taxpayer's Social Security Number _____ Spouse's Social Security Number _____

Present Home Address _____ City, State, Zip Code _____

E-Mail Address _____

Filing Status: Please Check One
☐ Single ☐ Married Filing Joint ☐ Married Filing Separately ☐ Head of Household ☐ Qualifying Widow(er)

If you selected head of household and have no dependents, list the name and Social Security number _____ of your qualified child who lives with you and qualifies you for this status.

Dependents/Nondependents Qualifying for Child Care and/or EIC
Note: If any children listed below are nondependents then mark an "X" in the column listed "Non Dep."

First Name	Last Name	Date of Birth	Social Security Number	Relationship	Months In home	Non Dep.

If you are claiming as a dependent a child who did not live with you, check the documents that substantiate this claim:
☐ Pre-1985 divorce or separation agreement ☐ Signed Form 8332
☐ Post-1984 divorce or separation agreement WITHOUT CONDITIONS

Taxpayer's Birth Date _____ Spouse's Birth Date _____

Taxpayer's Occupation _____ Spouse's Occupation _____

Daytime Phone _____ Daytime Phone _____

Evening Phone _____ Evening Phone _____

Cell/FAX Phone _____ Cell/FAX Phone _____

State of Residency (2-Letter Abbreviation) _____ State of Part-year Residency _____ 2nd State of Part-year Residency _____

Please use the following space for any comments you wish to make to your preparer.

_____
_____
_____
_____
_____
_____
_____

©2017 Universal Tax Systems, Inc. and/or its affiliates and licensors. All rights reserved. ORGGENS1

Question Page 1

A check off list to show the types of income received at any time during the year.

2017 TAX QUESTIONS

AT ANY TIME DURING 2017:

Did you or your spouse receive income from the following sources:

YES	NO	
		Wages?
		Tips?
		Interest or Dividends?
		Social Security or Tier I Railroad Retirement?
		Lump sum from an employer sponsored plan and the recipient and/or employee was born before 1936?
		Retirement or IRA distribution for which the recipient is under age 59 1/2?
		Other pension, annuity, IRA, or retirement income?
		If IRA distribution, were nondeductible contributions ever made?
		If yes, provide the balance of all IRA accounts as of the end of 2017.
		Unemployment compensation?
		Alimony?
		Self-employment and/or operation of a business?
		Operation of a farm?
		Rental of land and property for agricultural purposes?
		Other rental property?
		Gambling winnings?
		Royalties?
		Any miscellaneous income, such as prizes or jury duty pay?

Did you or your spouse receive any of the following forms: (Please provide them to your preparer)

YES	NO	
		W-2
		W-2G
		1095-A, 1095-B or 1095-C
		1099R
		1099INT
		1099DIV
		1099MISC
		1099B
		1099S
		1099G
		Any other 1099
		K-1
		IRS notice of change to prior year's return
		Closing statements from real estate sales, purchases, or refinancing

Did you or your spouse sell or dispose of any of the following property:

YES	NO	
		Stock, mutual fund, or other non-business assets?
		Your personal residence?
		Rental property?
		Property relating to a business or farm?
		Any other business property not listed above? (i.e. equipment, land)
		If you sold any property above, did it involve a bartering agreement?
		If you sold any property above, are you receiving payments in installments?

Question Page 2

2017 TAX QUESTIONS

AT ANY TIME DURING 2017:

Did you or your spouse

YES	NO	
		Have a home mortgage?
		Refinance your home mortgage?
		Use a portion of your home exclusively for business?
		Have medical expenses or pay for health insurance?
		Make regular or substantial contributions to charity, church, etc.?
		If yes, did you make over $500.00 in non-cash contributions?
		Suffer a loss as a result of a casualty (fire, theft, natural disaster, etc.)?
		Incur any out-of-pocket expenses or use your personal vehicle in conjunction with your job?
		Move to be closer to a new job?
		Send payments to the IRS/state in order to prepay your current year tax liability (estimated taxes) or apply an overpayment from 2016?
		Have any interest in a partnership or S-corporation, estate or trust for which you expect to receive Form K-1?
		Have any household employees to whom you paid $1000.00 or more?
		Have a qualified fuel tax credit?
		Contribute to an: ☐ IRA? ☐ SEP? ☐ Keogh? ☐ Roth? ☐ or Simple retirement plan?
		Get claimed (or were eligible to be claimed) as a dependent on anyone else's return?

YES	NO	
		Did your children receive more than $1,050 and less than $10,500 from interest and dividends that you wish to claim on your own tax return instead of your child's?
		Did you pay child or dependent care expenses? If so, please bring names, addresses, Social Security/EIN numbers, amount paid to each provider, and amount paid for each dependent.
		Did you pay qualified post-secondary education tuition and related expenses for yourself, your spouse, or your dependents?
		Did you cash any US EE or I bonds to pay for post-secondary education for yourself, your spouse, or your dependents?
		Did you pay interest on higher education loans?
		Were you a pre-college educator who purchased books or classroom supplies?
		Did you purchase a car, boat, aircraft, motor home or home building materials in 2017 or keep receipts on all sales tax items purchased in 2017?
		Were there any births, adoptions, divorces, marriages, or deaths in your household?
		Do you desire direct deposit? If yes, please attach voided check.

W-2 Income

List all of your employers including name, address, and employer identification number.

W-2 INCOME	2017 (W-2)

Listed below are your employers shown on your last year's income tax return.

Name of employer
Street address
City, State, Zip Code
Employer Identification Number

☐ TAXPAYER ☐ SPOUSE

Name of employer
Street address
City, State, Zip Code
Employer Identification Number

☐ TAXPAYER ☐ SPOUSE

Name of employer
Street address
City, State, Zip Code
Employer Identification Number

☐ TAXPAYER ☐ SPOUSE

Name of employer
Street address
City, State, Zip Code
Employer Identification Number

☐ TAXPAYER ☐ SPOUSE

Name of employer
Street address
City, State, Zip Code
Employer Identification Number

☐ TAXPAYER ☐ SPOUSE

Name of employer
Street address
City, State, Zip Code
Employer Identification Number

☐ TAXPAYER ☐ SPOUSE

Name of employer
Street address
City, State, Zip Code
Employer Identification Number

☐ TAXPAYER ☐ SPOUSE

Name of employer
Street address
City, State, Zip Code
Employer Identification Number

☐ TAXPAYER ☐ SPOUSE

* Please include a W-2 from each of your 2017 employers.

W-2G Income and Estimated Tax Paid

Include name of payer, address, TIN of all gambling winnings and quarterly tax payments.

W-2G INCOME

2018 (W-2G)

Listed below are payers shown on your last year's income tax return.
*Please include any W-2G from each of your 2018 payers.

Name of payer
Street address
City, State, Zip Code
Federal Identification Number

☐ TAXPAYER ☐ SPOUSE

Name of payer
Street address
City, State, Zip Code
Federal Identification Number

☐ TAXPAYER ☐ SPOUSE

Name of payer
Street address
City, State, Zip Code
Federal Identification Number

☐ TAXPAYER ☐ SPOUSE

ESTIMATED TAX PAID FOR THE 2018 TAX YEAR (FED/ST TAX)

* Please enter only the payments to be applied to the current year tax, including any payments made in January of 2019.

Federal payments		State of ___ payments	
Date paid	Amount paid	Date paid	Amount paid
_____	_____	_____	_____
_____	_____	_____	_____
_____	_____	_____	_____
_____	_____	_____	_____

State/local income tax balance due for previous years paid in 2018: _____

State/local estimate payment for 2017, due January 15, 2018, paid on or after January 1, 2018: _____

© 2017 Universal Tax Systems, Inc. and/or its affiliates and licensors. All rights reserved.

Other Income and Adjustments

Include state tax refund, unemployment, SE retirement, health insurance & IRA's.

OTHER INCOME AND ADJUSTMENTS				2018
OTHER INCOME			2018	2017
Seller Financed Mortgages				
Payer	Principal	Interest		Interest
_____	_____	_____		_____
_____	_____	_____		_____
_____	_____	_____		_____
_____	_____	_____		_____
_____	_____	_____		_____
_____	_____	_____		_____
_____	_____	_____		_____

State and Local Income Tax Refunds Received in 2018

State or Local jurisdiction _____ Amount received _____
State or Local jurisdiction _____ Amount received _____
State or Local jurisdiction _____ Amount received _____

Unemployment (Please attach 1099G(s))	2018	2017
Amount received:	_____	_____
Amount repaid:	_____	_____

Alimony amount received _____ _____

Other Income
Type: _____ Amount: _____ _____

ADJUSTMENTS	Taxpayer 2018	Taxpayer 2017	Spouse 2018	Spouse 2017
Educator expense	_____	_____	_____	_____
Self-employed retirement plans	_____	_____	_____	_____
Self-employed health insurance paid	_____	_____	_____	_____
IRA'S				
Traditional	_____	_____	_____	_____
Roth	_____	_____	_____	_____
Student loan interest	_____	_____	_____	_____

Alimony Paid
To whom paid: _____ Amount: _____ _____
SSN: _____

Tuition and Fees Amount: _____ _____

Other Adjustments
Type: _____ Amount: _____ _____

Interest and Dividend Income

List all income from forms 1099-INT & 1099-DIV.

INTEREST AND DIVIDEND INCOME			2017 (SCH B)
INTEREST INCOME		2017	2016
T,S,J*	NAME OF PAYER		
	If you received any interest income from a seller financed mortgage, please enter the payer's name, address, and their SSN or EIN.		
	Name	SSN/EIN	
	City, State, Zip	Amount	
____	Amount of nominee interest		
____	Amount of accrued interest		
____	Amount of tax-exempt interest		
____	Amount of OID adjustment		
____	Amount of ABP adjustment		
DIVIDEND INCOME		2017	2016
T,S,J*	NAME OF PAYER	ORDINARY	ORDINARY
	*Taxpayer, Spouse or Joint	Nominee Distribution Dividends	
	*Please attach any 1099-INT, 1099-OID, and 1099-DIV forms		

Pension and Retirement Income

List pension, IRA distributions, and social security received.

PENSION AND RETIREMENT INCOME — 2018 (1099R)

PENSIONS AND IRAS
Listed below are your pension, IRA distributions, and Social Security received last year (if any).

Payer 1
- Name of payer
- Street address
- City, State, Zip Code
- Employer Identification Number
- ☐ TAXPAYER ☐ SPOUSE ☐ IRA

Payer 2
- Name of payer
- Street address
- City, State, Zip Code
- Employer Identification Number
- ☐ TAXPAYER ☐ SPOUSE ☐ IRA

Payer 3
- Name of payer
- Street address
- City, State, Zip Code
- Employer Identification Number
- ☐ TAXPAYER ☐ SPOUSE ☐ IRA

Payer 4
- Name of payer
- Street address
- City, State, Zip Code
- Employer Identification Number
- ☐ TAXPAYER ☐ SPOUSE ☐ IRA

Payer 5
- Name of payer
- Street address
- City, State, Zip Code
- Employer Identification Number
- ☐ TAXPAYER ☐ SPOUSE ☐ IRA

Payer 6
- Name of payer
- Street address
- City, State, Zip Code
- Employer Identification Number
- ☐ TAXPAYER ☐ SPOUSE ☐ IRA

* Please include any 1099's and other 2018 information.
If you ever made non-deductible contributions to your IRA, please provide year-end balances of all your IRA accounts.

SOCIAL SECURITY BENEFITS (1040 WKT)

	2018 AMOUNTS	2017 TOTAL AMOUNT
Taxpayer Amount	$	
Spouse Amount	$	

© 2017 Universal Tax Systems, Inc. and/or its affiliates and licensors. All rights reserved.

Estate and Trust Income

Include your K-1 information such as name of estate or trust and federal ID number.

ESTATE AND TRUST INCOME
2018 (K-1 E/T)

Your 2017 K-1 information is shown below.

K-1 INFORMATION

Name of Estate, Trust
Federal ID Number
If any rental real estate, are you an active participant?

K-1 INFORMATION

Name of Estate, Trust
Federal ID Number
If any rental real estate, are you an active participant?

K-1 INFORMATION

Name of Estate, Trust
Federal ID Number
If any rental real estate, are you an active participant?

K-1 INFORMATION

Name of Estate, Trust
Federal ID Number
If any rental real estate, are you an active participant?

K-1 INFORMATION

Name of Estate, Trust
Federal ID Number
If any rental real estate, are you an active participant?

K-1 INFORMATION

Name of Estate, Trust
Federal ID Number
If any rental real estate, are you an active participant?

K-1 INFORMATION

Name of Estate, Trust
Federal ID Number
If any rental real estate, are you an active participant?

K-1 INFORMATION

Name of Estate, Trust
Federal ID Number
If any rental real estate, are you an active participant?

K-1 INFORMATION

Name of Estate, Trust
Federal ID Number
If any rental real estate, are you an active participant?

* Please attach all K-1 schedules received for 2018.

Capital Gains and Losses

List all stocks and non-business asset sales, with description, date acquired, sold, sales price & cost.

CAPITAL GAINS AND LOSSES				2017 (SCH D)
Stocks, Bonds, and Non-Business Assets				
Description	Date Acquired	Date Sold	Sales Price	Cost

Amount of short-term loss carryover from 2016 _____

Amount of long-term loss carryover from 2016 _____

Business Income and Expenses (Sch C)

Input self-employed income with name, tax ID, address, start date and income & expenses.

BUSINESS INCOME AND EXPENSES — 2018 (SCH C)

Your principal business or profession _____   Is this your spouse's Schedule C? _____

Business name _____   2017 Business code _____

Business address _____   Employer ID _____
(Not SSN)
Accounting method: _____

Enter date if you disposed of or sold this business during the year _____

BUSINESS VEHICLE	2018	2017
Date placed in service _____		
Miles used for: Business		
Commuting		
Other		
PART I INCOME		
Gross receipts or sales		
Returns and allowances		
Other income		
PART II EXPENSES		
Advertising		
Car/Truck expenses		
Commissions		
Contract labor		
Depletion		
Employee benefit programs		
Insurance		
Interest - mortgage		
Interest - other		
Legal and professional services		
Office expense		
Pension and profit sharing		
Rent or lease - vehicles, machinery		
Rent - Other business property		
Repairs and maintenance		
Supplies		
Taxes and licenses		
Travel		
Meals and entertainment		
Utilities		
Wages		
Enter prior year unallowed loss (if any)		
OTHER EXPENSES		(SCH C PG 2)
_____		
_____		
_____		
_____		
_____		
_____		
_____		

Inventory method: ☐ Cost ☐ Lower of Cost or Market ☐ Other
Inventory at beginning of year
Purchases less cost of personal items
Inventory at end of year

Office in Home Deduction

List sq ft of total home vs area used for business, mortgage interest, rent, taxes, insurance & utilities.

OFFICE IN THE HOME DEDUCTION	2017	2017 (8829)
		2016
Square footage of area used for business		
Total square footage in your home		
Is this your spouse's Schedule C?		
Day care facilities:		
Number of days used for day care		
Number of hours per day used for day care		
Enter date if you disposed of or sold this business during the year		
EXPENSES DIRECTLY RELATING TO YOUR BUSINESS	**2017**	**2016**
Casualty losses		
Deductible mortgage interest		
Real estate taxes		
Insurance		
Rent		
Repairs and maintenance		
Utilities		
Other expenses		
EXPENSES RELATING TO ENTIRE HOUSEHOLD		
Casualty losses		
Deductible mortgage interest		
Real estate taxes		
Insurance		
Rent		
Repairs and maintenance		
Utilities		
Other expenses		
Carryover of operating expenses from 2016 Form 8829 line 42		
Carryover of excess casualty losses and depreciation from 2016 Form 8829 line 43		
Enter the fair market value of your home		
Enter the cost of your home		
Enter the value of the land on which your home is placed		

Business Asset List

List business assets with description, date acquired & sold, cost, sales price & prior depreciation schedule.

BUSINESS ASSET LIST 2017

Asset acquisition list (Please list all assets you have purchased or placed in service in 2017.)

Description	Date Acquired	Cost	To Schedule

Asset disposition list (Please list all assets you sold, traded, junked, or took out of service for any reason in 2017.)

Description	Date Acquired	Date Sold	Sales Price	Sales Expenses	Cost	Prior Depreciation	From Sch.

© 2017 Universal Tax Systems, Inc. and/or its affiliates and licensors. All rights reserved.

ORGASSET

Itemized Deductions

List medical, dental, taxes, interest, and charitable expenses.

ITEMIZED DEDUCTIONS			2018 (SCH A)
	*T,S,J	2018	2017
MEDICAL AND DENTAL EXPENSES - Include prescription medicine & drugs, nonprescription medical supplies such as crutches, doctors, dentists, nurses, hospitals, medical insurance premiums, medical miles or actual expense."			
Number of medical miles			
* Do not list amounts paid with pre-tax dollars or that were reimbursed.			
* Taxpayer, Spouse, or Joint			
TAXES PAID			
Real estate taxes			
Personal property taxes			
Other_____			
INTEREST PAID			
Home mortgage interest			
Points paid in purchasing new home			
Investment interest expense			
CONTRIBUTIONS - Receipts required for all contributions			
Cash			
Non-cash			
Number of charity miles			

Rental Income and Expenses (Schedule E)

List all income, expense and property details for real estate rentals.

RENTAL REAL ESTATE AND ROYALTIES						2017 (SCH E)	
	Property A		Property B		Property C		
KIND OF PROPERTY							
LOCATION OF PROPERTY							
CITY							
STATE							
ZIP							
INCOME	2017	2016	2017	2016	2017	2016	
Rent received							
Royalties received							
EXPENSES							
Advertising							
Auto and travel							
Cleaning and maintenance							
Commissions							
Insurance							
Legal, professional fees							
Management fees							
Mortgage interest							
Other interest							
Repairs							
Supplies							
Taxes							
Utilities							
Miscellaneous Expenses							
Type of misc expense 1							
Amount Item 1							
Type of misc expense 2							
Amount Item 2							
Type of misc expense 3							
Amount Item 3							
Type of misc expense 4							
Amount Item 4							
Enter loss carryover to 2017							
Did you actively participate in this venture?							
Did you use this property for personal use?							

Child and Dependent Care Expenses

List care providers, amounts paid per child. Include name, address, EIN & telephone number.

CHILD AND DEPENDENT CARE EXPENSES — 2018 (2441)

Please list all care providers and the amounts paid to them in 2018. Any information from the prior year is shown below.

Name of provider
Street address
City, State, Zip Code
Social Security Number or EIN
Amount paid $ _____ 2017 AMOUNT $ _____

Name of provider
Street address
City, State, Zip Code
Social Security Number or EIN
Amount paid $ _____ 2017 AMOUNT $ _____

Name of provider
Street address
City, State, Zip Code
Social Security Number or EIN
Amount paid $ _____ 2017 AMOUNT $ _____

Name of provider
Street address
City, State, Zip Code
Social Security Number or EIN
Amount paid $ _____ 2017 AMOUNT $ _____

Name of provider
Street address
City, State, Zip Code
Social Security Number or EIN
Amount paid $ _____ 2017 AMOUNT $ _____

List name of each child and total amount spent for care of that child.

_____ $ _____
_____ $ _____
_____ $ _____
_____ $ _____

PRO-FORMA TAX ORGANIZER

A pro-forma tax organizer will have all of your prior year income and deductions carried forward and listed. This is helpful so you will know exactly what you normally have and are less likely to forget anything.

I am happy to help you with your tax organizer, or if you have any other questions and concerns or need any bookkeeping services. Please use the contact form at bookkeeping-basics.net/contact-me.html and put your question in the comment area. I will not be able to answer all questions, but will do my best.

Also feel free to let me know what you think of my website. Is it suiting your needs? Is there anything else you need help with and would like to see added?

I'm always delighted to get your feedback!

EXCEL TAX WORKSHEETS

Help Get Started

*Help others achieve their dreams
and you will achieve yours.
—Les Brown*

THERE ARE CONVENIENT EXCEL tax worksheets available that are great when you don't want to spend a lot of money on accounting software when getting started putting together your income and expenses.

Rather than having to purchase software such as QuickBooks, you can get started right away with the excel software you already have utilizing free and inexpensive excel bookkeeping templates and spreadsheets for sole proprietor schedule C or rental real estate transactions

BALANCE SHEET

The first excel template is free and offers an outline of all of the typical accounts you might find on a basic balance sheet report.

You can simply fill in your own information in column D as necessary. There are already some formulas built right in, but you can add additional formulas as well.

Please feel free to use the balance sheet worksheet by changing it, spicing it up with the different formatting features, adding more complicated formulas, etc...

In fact you're welcome to use all of the bookkeeping templates you find here in any way that suits your needs.

SMALL PROFIT AND LOSS

This excel bookkeeping template is the first Excel Spreadsheet Profit and Loss under 50 transactions and is for small start-up sole proprietor business owners reporting as a Schedule C on their tax returns.

If you are a business with a low number of monthly and annual transactions, you may wish to purchase this easy to use Excel Sole Proprietor Spreadsheet to enter your transactions instead of more costly software such as QuickBooks. This will help you to save money as you are getting started.

The spreadsheet is setup with separate tabs for Cost of Goods Sold, Income, General Expenses and Other Expenses where you can enter your daily or monthly transactions with subtotals and totals and links to a profit and loss report all built right in for you.

It is all set and ready to go, no need for formatting and you can easily enter any additional categories needed as well. It can be well worth the money especially when comparing to software such as QuickBooks that can cost over $200.

LARGE PROFIT AND LOSS

This second Excel Spreadsheet Profit and Loss under 100 transactions is for mid-size businesses with over 50 and under 100 transactions. With this you get even more for your money.

The spreadsheet is also setup with separate tabs for Cost of Goods Sold, Income, General Expenses and Other Expenses where you can enter your daily or monthly transactions with subtotals and totals and links to a profit and loss report all built right in for you.

Everything here is all set and ready to go as well, including printing setup and instructions on how to enter your daily activities.

You can get the excel balance sheet and profit & loss worksheets at bookkeeping-basics.net/excel-bookkeeping-template.html

All the best to you!

If you enjoyed reading this book, I'd appreciate it if you would take a couple of minutes to post a short review at Amazon. Intelligent reviews help other customers make better buying choices. And because I read all my reviews personally, they will help me to write better books in the future. Thanks for your support!

ADDITIONAL RESOURCES

YOUTUBE: youtube.com/user/hornefinancial

PINTEREST: pinterest.com/hornefncl

TWITTER: twitter.com/hornefncl

SMASHWORDS: smashwords.com/interview/hornefinancial

AMAZON: https://www.amazon.com/author/stephaniehorne

AMAZON BOOK: Accounting For Small Business

AMAZON BOOK: Bookkeeping 101 For Business Professionals

AMAZON BOOK: Small Business Accounting 101

GLOSSARY: bookkeeping-basics.net/accounting-definitions-glossary.html

WORD SEARCH: bookkeeping-basics.net/accounting-definitions-word-search.html

E-COURSE: bookkeeping-basics.net/accounting-definitions-ecourse.html

NOTES

www.ingramcontent.com/pod-product-compliance
Lightning Source LLC
Chambersburg PA
CBHW031427210526
45464CB00005B/2086